OF EMBODIED PRESENCE
AND THE ACTOR'S ASCENT THROUGH
INTEGRATIVE PRACTICES AND TRANSPERSONAL WISDOM

ROOTING

AWAKENING

TRANSCENDING

JIAWEI LIU, PH.D

1 PLUS BOOKS

1 Plus Books
http://1plusbooks.com

Author：Jiawei Liu, Ph.D
Title：Rooting Awakening Transcending
Subtitle: Of Embodied Presence and the Actor's Ascent
through Integrative Practices and Transpersonal Wisdom

©2025 Jiawei Liu
2025 1 Plus Books®
Paperback Edition
Published and Printed in the United States of America

ISBN: 978-1-966814-08-5

Publisher：Yan Liu
Book Design: 1 Plus Books
Suggested Retail Price：$19.99

San Francisco, USA , 2025
https://1plusbooks.com
email: 1plus@1plusbooks.com

Dedication

To my dearest Kathy,

Thou art the quiet force that steadies our home, the unwavering heart that bore its weight while my spirit wandered in the realm of creation. No words may encompass the breadth of my gratitude, nor can my pen trace the depth of thy sacrifice. So I lay before thee this book—not in measure, but in reverence—a humble offering of my boundless love, my endless thanks, and the silent verses of devotion that ever dwell within me.

About the Author

Jiawei Liu holds a Bachelor of Arts in Theatre Performance from Shanghai Theatre Academy, a Master of Arts in Theatre Directing from Moscow State University of Arts, a Master of Arts in Multimedia Communications from the Academy of Art University, and a PhD in Transpersonal Psychology from Sofia University. He is the Executive Vice President of Golden Gate College, a Board Member of California Private University, and Chair of the Drama and Psychology Association under the Da Vinci Education Foundation. His published works, including Training Language for Directing and Acting, On the Stage, and Transpersonal Methods in Actor Training, explore the theoretical and practical intersections of acting and psychology. His scholarly contributions, featured in journals such as Art Evaluation and Drama House, reflect a sustained engagement with performance studies and psychological inquiry. Liu's contributions extend beyond scholarship to innovation, holding patents for an Intelligent Sandplay Device and a Dramatic Performance Display System, both exemplifying his commitment to advancing the field. His original theatrical works, such as Moving and The Sage Confucius, further demonstrate his synthesis of psychological insight with creative practice, positioning him as a significant voice in the evolving dialogue between psychology and the performing arts.

Acknowledgements

No work is ever truly the labor of one. Every endeavor, every creation, is shaped by the unseen hands and quiet sacrifices of others—those who stand beside us, believing when we doubt, uplifting when we falter, and offering their strength when our own wanes. This book, though bound in my name, is the culmination of a shared journey, one that I did not and could not walk alone. To those who have walked it with me, I offer not just my gratitude, but my deepest reverence.

Before all else, my deepest gratitude belongs to my father, Qiang Liu. It is often said that behind every pursuit of knowledge and every realized dream stands an unwavering supporter, someone who provides not only encouragement but also the means to turn vision into reality. My father has been that pillar for me. His support was not just financial—it was an unspoken belief in my work, a quiet assurance that my ideas deserved to be explored, developed, and shared with the world. His generosity extended beyond material resources; it was a gift of trust, a silent yet profound acknowledgment that this journey was worth undertaking. To him, I owe not just this book, but the very foundation upon which it stands.

I extend my profound appreciation to Dr. George Guim, a mentor whose wisdom and generosity have left an indelible imprint upon both this work and myself. His meticulous guidance, his keen intellect, and his unwavering support through the intricacies of experimental design and textual refinement have been invaluable. More than a scholar, he has been a steady presence, ensuring that this book is not only a product of inquiry but of integrity. To him, I owe more than thanks—I owe the very foundation upon which this research stands.

Equally, I am deeply indebted to the volunteers who lent their time, their trust, and their very selves to this study. Research is more than data points and measured outcomes—it is the willingness of individuals to step forward, to open themselves to the unknown, and in doing so, illuminate truths that would otherwise remain obscured. To each participant, I offer my sincerest gratitude. This book carries your voices within its pages, and it is as much yours as it is mine.

To Dr. Jet Hermes, my esteemed friend and the author of this book's foreword, I owe a debt of gratitude beyond words. He is not only a psychologist of exceptional skill but a man whose journey into the field was shaped by the crucible of personal experience. Born in the vibrant city of Guangzhou, fluent in both Cantonese and Mandarin, his formative years were marked by hardship—an early encounter with suffering that ignited in him a lifelong pursuit of healing, first for himself, and then for others. His dedication led him to earn a Doctorate of Psychology (Psy.D.) from Sofia University, where he refined his expertise in Internal Family Systems (IFS), Psychodrama, Gestalt Group Work, and Past-Life Regression Therapy. For those drawn to more structured approaches, he is also adept in Cognitive Behavioral Therapy (CBT), Dialectical Behavior Therapy (DBT), and Acceptance and Commitment Therapy (ACT). Yet, beyond his vast professional expertise, it is his unwavering kindness, his quiet but steadfast belief in the transformative power of this book, that humbles me most. In the midst of his own work—work that changes lives—he found time to lend his voice to mine. That is a gift beyond measure, and one I will never forget.

But gratitude, in its truest form, extends beyond professional guidance; it is found in the quiet sanctuaries of home, in the gentle care of those who ask for nothing in return, who give not out of obligation but out of love. To my brothers in heart and spirit—Stone (Sitong Qian), Zhongnan Luo, Wenhao Chen, and Lilly Yan—I extend not just thanks, but the deepest appreciation of a soul sustained. Stone, with his culinary artistry, ensured that no evening passed without warmth and nourishment, his meals a quiet reminder that care can be tasted, that love can be found in something as simple as a bowl of rice. Wenhao, with his tireless dedication, tended to the unseen burdens of daily life—cleaning, tidying, restoring order to the spaces I left in creative disarray. Zhongnan Luo, with his gentle watchfulness, cared for my child as though he were his own, offering me the rarest of gifts: peace of mind. And Lilly Yan, with the grace of one who knows that love is often found in the smallest gestures, prepared shrimp wontons with a delicacy that was not only nourishing but deeply comforting—a taste of home, of care woven into every fold. These are the people who remind me that family is not bound by blood alone, but by the kindness that lingers long after the meal is eaten, after the room is cleaned, after the day is done.

And then, there are those whose love transcends words, whose presence is as constant as the stars. To three extraordinary women—my mother, Cao Lin; Dr. Liz Li, President of Golden Gate College; and

May Zhong—I owe a gratitude beyond what language can hold. My mother, my first teacher, my unwavering anchor, has given me the kind of love that asks for nothing yet gives everything. It is her quiet strength, her unshaken belief in me, that has carried me through every moment of doubt. Dr. Liz Li, with a kindness that knows no bounds, stood by my side through illness and surgery, her care a light in what could have been darkness. May Zhong, with hands that never tired, with a heart that never wavered, ensured that I was not only looked after but truly seen, truly cared for. These women have given of themselves in ways that can never be repaid, only honored. And so I honor them here, in these words, though words will never be enough.

Finally, to my family and friends, who have been the silent architects of my perseverance, I offer my deepest thanks. It is their belief in me, even when my own wavered, that carried me to this moment. This book is not solely mine—it is a testament to their love, their patience, their quiet sacrifices. To each of them, I say this: whatever merit lies within these pages, it is as much yours as it is mine.

With the fullness of my heart, I dedicate these words to you.

Abstract

The Transpersonal Actor:
Illuminating the Actor's Inner Landscape through
Transpersonal Consciousness Practices

What truly defines an exceptional performance? Beyond technical mastery and emotional expression, is there an inner dimension that can elevate an actor's craft? This book explores the profound intersection between transpersonal psychology and drama, investigating how psychological methods rooted in mindfulness and embodied awareness can deepen an actor's connection to their role, refine their presence on stage, and ultimately transform their approach to performance.

At the core of this study is the application of transpersonal psychological techniques—specifically aikido and mindfulness meditation—within actor training. Conducted at Sofia University, the research was designed to examine the impact of these methods from two primary perspectives: first, assessing the direct influence of transpersonal practices on acting performance; and second, analyzing how individual factors such as professional training, gender, cultural background, and age shape the effectiveness of these interventions.

The study followed a structured four-step process. Initially, participants performed without any psychological intervention, and their performances were evaluated by an audience. This was followed by an intensive period of transpersonal training, where participants engaged in aikido and mindfulness meditation under the guidance of professional instructors. After this intervention, participants performed once again, with their second performances re-evaluated to measure changes. Finally, participants completed questionnaires detailing their personal experiences and perceptions of the psychological training.

The results were both compelling and revealing. Across the board, actors demonstrated higher performance scores after engaging in transpersonal practices, indicating an enhanced capacity for embodiment, presence, and emotional expression. Furthermore, variations emerged based on individual conditions. Experienced actors showed a greater ability to integrate these techniques into their craft compared to beginners. Female participants displayed stronger responses to the interventions than their male counterparts. Those from Eastern cultural backgrounds exhibited greater receptivity to the practices compared to those from Western backgrounds. Additionally, actors between the ages of 35 and 50 demonstrated more pronounced benefits than younger participants.

These findings hold significant implications for the future of actor training. They suggest that beyond traditional performance techniques, integrating transpersonal psychological methods can offer actors a pathway to greater self-awareness, emotional depth, and artistic authenticity. This book extends beyond the empirical study to explore how such practices can be implemented in acting pedagogy, opening new possibilities for both performers and educators.

By bridging psychology and performance, this work offers not only a scholarly contribution to the fields of transpersonal psychology and drama but also a practical guide for actors seeking a more profound engagement with their craft. Through an exploration of mind-body integration, presence, and the fluidity of consciousness, it presents a transformative approach to performance—one that transcends mere technique and touches the very essence of artistic expression.

Preface

What is acting, really? To me, it defies rigid categories and absolute definitions. If we must define it, perhaps we are actually discussing "you," "me," and "them." Life itself is a constellation of fragmented moments, and if we attempt to deconstruct these moments with the rigor of a philosopher, we may never settle on a singular meaning of existence. Yet, as actors, these moments—these lived experiences— become our artistic canvas. They are internalized, transformed, and ultimately externalized through our bodies, voices, and expressions, breathing vitality into the characters we embody.

This is why we act, why we train, and why we embark on the perpetual search for those unfiltered, visceral emotions that reside deep within us. And this is why I wrote this book. My objective is to introduce two unconventional yet profoundly effective training methods, drawn from the principles of transpersonal psychology, to help actors deepen their understanding of selfhood. By starting with this fundamental premise, we can revolutionize the way we approach acting training and, ultimately, redefine our understanding of performance itself. My hope is that all those who are passionate about acting—and, more broadly, about life—will come to view performance not merely as a technical skill, but as a deeply integrated aspect of human existence.

About six years ago, while living in San Francisco, I frequently attended rehearsals at local amateur theater groups. During this time, I befriended a visual artist who had rented an office in a small institution in Palo Alto called Sofia University. It was through him that I first encountered the university—and, more crucially, the field of transpersonal psychology. Until that moment, I had never considered that psychology could extend beyond the confines of behavior and cognition into the realm of the transcendent. Driven by an insatiable intellectual curiosity and a deep reverence for psychology's potential, I pursued a doctoral degree in transpersonal psychology at Sofia University—a decision that would profoundly reshape my perspective on acting.

Acting and psychology are inextricably linked. Our craft is, at its core, the art of navigating the depths of human consciousness. As I immersed myself in transpersonal psychology, my understanding of the self expanded beyond conventional paradigms. I began to question: Is acting an objective craft, reducible to technique and methodology? Or is it an inherently subjective, deeply personal process, one that requires the actor to summon their own consciousness and extend it beyond the self? Are actors merely replicating external behaviors in a detached manner, or are they channeling something far more intrinsic and transformative?

Through this inquiry, I arrived at a pivotal realization: acting is not merely an artistic pursuit—it is a process of psychological evolution. When actors fully engage with a role, they transcend their individual identities, dissolving the boundaries of selfhood in order to inhabit something greater than themselves. It is in this liminal space between self and other that the most profound performances take shape.

How, then, can actors more effectively access this state? How can they move beyond the constraints of technical execution and instead cultivate a state of being that allows for the seamless flow of life energy within their performance? These questions form the foundation of this book.

If you believe acting is simply the mastery of lines, emotions, and movement, you may be overlooking its deeper dimensions. Consider this: Aikido, a Japanese martial art, may seem entirely unrelated to acting—yet it holds the key to unlocking an actor's sense of rhythm and spatial awareness. In Aikido, force is not met with resistance but with redirection; the practitioner learns to attune themselves to the energy of their opponent and move in harmony with it. Is this not precisely what great actors do? Onstage, actors must be attuned to the energy of their scene partners, the audience, and the environment itself. Performance is not simply about speaking or moving—it is about navigating the invisible currents of energy that shape the dramatic moment.

And what of mindfulness meditation? Imagine an actor standing center stage, enveloped in a tempest of emotion, yet maintaining an unwavering inner stillness. Actors are not passive vessels for emotion; they are active architects of presence. They must simultaneously immerse themselves in the world of their characters while maintaining a heightened awareness of self. Meditation cultivates this dual awareness, allowing actors to fully experience emotion without being engulfed by it. Rather than being swept away by feeling, they learn to harness it, refining every breath, every micro-expression, every energetic shift.

This may sound unconventional—perhaps even radical—but that is precisely what makes it so compelling. Acting is not a static art; it is a living, breathing exploration of human consciousness. If you have ever been spellbound by a performance, unable to articulate exactly why, it was likely because the actor was weaving something beyond the visible, something that transcended spoken language and gesture.

They were sculpting presence itself.

Thus, acting can be cultivated like a martial art, refined like a meditative practice, and experienced like an altered state of consciousness. A truly exceptional actor does not merely execute movements or recite dialogue; they engage with the unseen forces of space, rhythm, and energy. They transform the very air within a theater, drawing the audience into a collective, immersive experience.

This book, then, is not simply about acting methodology—it is an exploration of the psyche. Within these pages, you will discover how transpersonal psychology offers actors a means of transcending conventional training methods, allowing for performances that are not only more compelling but also more authentic. This is a book for those who seek to unlock the deeper dimensions of performance, not just as an art form, but as a profound vehicle for self-discovery.

When actors respond to the call of a higher self, they step into their fullest potential. This is not merely an enhancement of technique; it is a transformation of being. Through acting, performers cultivate transpersonal qualities—openness, empathy, forgiveness, compassion, a sense of justice, a redefined sense of self, and even an expanded awareness of the interconnectedness of all things. These attributes elevate the actor from an isolated individual to a vital participant in a greater, shared reality. No longer confined to the realm of "I," they become an integral part of "us."

When an actor breaks free from the constraints of personal identity and embraces the concept of unity, they transcend the limits of the individual self. In that moment, they cease to be mere storytellers; they become the story itself. They do not simply portray a character—they embody it, dissolve into it, and breathe it into existence.

The pinnacle of acting is not in pretending to be someone else, but in discovering new dimensions of oneself within the character. Only by expanding beyond the personal into the transpersonal can actors craft performances that resonate on the deepest levels of human experience.

This book is dedicated to every actor, whether at the beginning of their journey or well along the path of artistic and personal transformation. I believe acting is not just a mode of artistic expression; it is an intimate inquiry into the psyche. My hope is that these pages illuminate a path toward a more profound understanding of acting and that, both on stage and in life, you discover the most authentic version of yourself.

Liu Jiawei, Ph.D.
Fremont, California
March 3, 2025

Foreword: The Art of Becoming

We live in a world of ceaseless motion, shifting between roles—professional, familial, social—rarely questioning the scripts we follow. From the moment we enter society, we are given lines to recite, gestures to perform, and masks to wear. We construct an identity that fits within these expectations, yet somewhere beneath the rehearsed expressions and learned behaviors lies a deeper question: Who am I beyond the roles I play? If life is a stage, then where does performance end and the authentic self begin?

This question is not new. For centuries, philosophers, artists, and psychologists have pondered the nature of identity and transformation. But nowhere is this question more vividly explored than in the realm of acting. Why do some performers, after immersing themselves in a role, find it impossible to return to who they once were? Why does embodying another's existence so often reshape their own? The greatest actors do not merely portray emotions; they inhabit them. They dissolve into the experience so completely that the boundaries between self and character blur. And if a performance can alter the psychology of the performer, what does this tell us about the nature of selfhood?

Dr. Liu Jiawei, an accomplished scholar in both theater and psychology, takes these questions beyond philosophical reflection and into rigorous scientific inquiry. Trained at the Shanghai Theatre Academy and the Moscow State Institute of Theatre Arts, later earning his doctorate in Transpersonal Psychology from Sofia University, USA, Dr. Liu has spent years studying the intersection of performance and psychological transformation. His work challenges conventional notions of acting as mere imitation. Instead, he reveals that the stage is not just a place for storytelling—it is a space where identity is tested, reshaped, and sometimes entirely redefined.

Consider an actor standing alone on a dimly lit stage. The silence is vast, yet charged with possibility. At this moment, their body is no longer just an instrument of movement—it is a vessel of consciousness, a bridge between the physical and the intangible. Each breath is intentional, each gesture a revelation. They are not merely playing a role; they are stepping into being. When performance reaches this depth, it is no longer an act of mimicry but an act of becoming. The most extraordinary performances are not those in which actors "convince" the audience of their role, but those in which they uncover something real within themselves—something previously unspoken, unknown.

And when an actor experiences this, the audience does as well. In the stillness between words, in the smallest of gestures, something shifts. The illusion of separation dissolves, and what emerges is not just a character but a mirror—one that reflects back to the audience their own emotions, their own memories, their own yearning for authenticity. This is why theater has endured for millennia: it does not merely entertain; it awakens.

Dr. Liu's research is more than a theoretical examination of acting; it is an exploration of the fundamental mechanisms of human experience. Through experimental studies, he investigates how transpersonal psychological techniques—such as Aikido, mindfulness meditation, and embodied awareness practices—affect actors' ability to access emotion, presence, and truth. His findings demonstrate that these practices do not simply enhance performance; they cultivate a deeper connection between mind and body, allowing actors to reach levels of expression that are impossible through technique alone.

But what makes Dr. Liu's work even more compelling is that its implications extend beyond the theater. His research suggests that acting is not just an artistic discipline—it is a method of self-exploration, a tool for understanding the self beyond the limitations imposed by habit, memory, and societal expectation. If an actor can step onto a stage and temporarily dissolve into another existence, does this not reveal something profound about human potential? If identity can be stretched, reshaped, and even transcended through performance, what does this mean for how we live our daily lives?

Perhaps we are all, in some way, performing. The roles we adopt in our careers, our relationships, and our communities may be no different from those played on stage. But the question is not whether we are performing—it is whether we are aware of it. Are we passively reciting lines we were given, or are we actively shaping the narrative of our own becoming?

This book is not only for actors. It is an invitation to anyone who seeks to engage with life more fully, to strip away the layers of pretense, and to stand, even for a moment, in the pure clarity of presence. Acting, as Dr. Liu presents it, is not a departure from reality but a return to it. It is a practice of presence, a discipline of awareness, and ultimately, a path toward greater authenticity.

As the lights dim and the curtain rises, we find ourselves not in a theater, but in the unfolding drama of our own existence. Every breath, every movement, every decision is part of this great performance. And the choice before us is simple yet profound: Will we live as spectators, or will we step fully into the roles that only we can play?

The world is waiting. The stage is yours. Step forward—not just as an actor, but as a being fully alive.

— *Dr. Jet Hermes, Psy.D.*
Licensed Psychologist

Table of Contents

Chapter 1

The Intersection of Transpersonal Psychology and Performance

The Fusion of Mind and Art: A Journey Begins

Transpersonal psychology emerged in the mid-1960s as an extension of humanistic psychology, positioning itself as the fourth force in psychological inquiry following behaviorism, psychoanalysis, and humanistic psychology (Scotton, 1996). The foundational premise of humanistic psychology postulated that human existence was structured along three primary dimensions—physiological, emotional, and rational—which were interdependent and collectively manifested within the individual's psychological totality. However, despite its significance as an epistemological shift in psychological thought, humanistic psychology remained constrained by its emphasis on individualism, failing to account for the broader existential and transpersonal dimensions of human experience.

Critiques of these limitations emerged within academic discourse, particularly in the recognition that humanistic psychology's emphasis on self-actualization did not adequately encompass the full spectrum of human consciousness and transcendence. Frank (1978) posited that a defining characteristic of human nature was its inherent propensity for self-transcendence—an existential imperative that compels individuals to seek meaning beyond personal gratification, whether through acts of sacrifice, relational depth, or devotion to a greater purpose.

Frank (1978) asserted that authentic personhood is realized only in moments of self-exceedance, whereby an individual transcends the confines of the self to engage with a broader ontological reality (p. 53).

As theoretical discourse evolved, increasing scholarly attention was directed toward critiquing the limitations of humanistic psychology's individualism, leading to the emergence of a conceptual framework that linked personal development to an external, transcendental reality. This epistemological expansion—the recognition of a realm beyond individual selfhood—was pivotal in laying the groundwork for transpersonal psychology.

Theoretical Foundations of Transpersonal Psychology

Transpersonal psychology is characterized by its focus on psychological development beyond conventional, personal, or individualistic paradigms (Scotton, 1996). The discipline is predicated upon a conceptual shift from self-centered psychological models toward an orientation that acknowledges a transcendent, universal consciousness. Within this framework, the "transpersonal" is conceptualized as a catalyst for identity formation and existential awareness, encompassing states of consciousness that transcend the ego-bound self.

Unlike traditional psychological frameworks, transpersonal psychology seeks to synthesize spiritual traditions with empirical inquiry, integrating philosophical and contemplative traditions within the theoretical and methodological frameworks of modern psychology. By employing contemporary psychological models to elucidate the phenomenology of spiritual experience, transpersonal psychology bridges scientific inquiry and existential philosophy in a manner that reframes traditional notions of human consciousness.

A central tenet of transpersonal psychology is its emphasis on spirituality as a fundamental component of human experience. Maslow (1976) argued that spirituality constitutes an intrinsic dimension of human identity, integral to both self-concept and existential purpose. From this perspective, spirituality is not merely an abstract construct but a constitutive element of psychological wholeness, shaping self-perception, intersubjectivity, and modes of being (p. 108). This perspective has gained increasing acceptance within psychological scholarship, with transpersonal psychologists recognizing spirituality as a foundational determinant of psychological well-being and self-differentiation.

Embodied Practices in Transpersonal Psychology: Aikido and Mindfulness

Among the methodologies that operationalize transpersonal psychology, aikido and mindfulness meditation serve as embodied practices that facilitate transpersonal awareness. Aikido, a Japanese martial art, is distinguished by its integration of physical movement, energetic flo , and self-transcendence. Unlike conventional martial disciplines that emphasize combative efficac , aikido is predicated upon the harmonization of opposing forces, illustrating a philosophical paradigm of integration rather than opposition.

Mindfulness meditation, by contrast, is a cognitive and attentional practice that cultivates meta-awareness, emotional regulation, and self-reflexivit . The practice is characterized by the intentional redirection of cognitive focus toward present-moment awareness, achieved through a nonjudgmental and observational stance (Chiesa, Calati, & Serretti, 2011). Linehan (1994) describes mindfulness as the ability to observe both internal and external experiences without engaging in automatic reactivity or attachment, thereby fostering psychological equanimity.

Research has demonstrated that mindfulness facilitates a shift in attentional control, enabling individuals to experience a heightened state of cognitive flexibility and emotional resilience. Kabat-Zinn (1994) further asserts that mindfulness meditation enables a non-reactive stance toward momentary experiences, cultivating openness, curiosity, and acceptance as fundamental psychological dispositions (p. 15; Bishop et al., 2004). Within this framework, meditative practices operate as mechanisms of cognitive restructuring, allowing practitioners to reframe their perceptual engagement with reality (Kabat-Zinn, 2003).

Performance as a Psychological and Embodied Phenomenon

Theatrical performance is an inherently cognitive, emotional, and physiological process, requiring an actor's ability to synthesize technical skill with psychological depth. Performance necessitates a state of embodied transformation, wherein actors undergo a phenomenological shift in identity, assuming roles that necessitate both affective attunement and behavioral modulation. The efficacy of a performance is contingent upon an actor's capacity for presence, improvisation, and psychological integration, all of which are directly influenced by internal psychological states and external environmental stimuli.

Performance outcomes are not solely determined by technical skill but are heavily modulated by psychological variables. Actors frequently experience cognitive load, emotional regulation challenges, and physiological arousal states, all of which affect performance efficac . Frank and Jeffrey (2010) argue that performance outcomes are contingent upon an actor's ability to engage in crisis management, stress regulation, creative problem-solving, and emotional containment (p. 103). Empirical findings suggest that pre-performance anxiety correlates with elevated physiological arousal, reinforcing the significance of psychological training in actor preparation.

The intersection of psychology and performance studies has underscored the necessity of integrating transpersonal methodologies into actor training. By employing meditative practices and embodied disciplines, performers can cultivate attentional regulation, emotional resilience, and cognitive flexibilit , thereby enhancing expressivity and stage presence.

The Scope of This Inquiry

This book examines the integration of transpersonal psychology within theatrical performance, exploring the efficacy of aikido and mindfulness meditation as training modalities for actors. By analyzing the impact of transpersonal interventions on acting methodology, this study seeks to illuminate how transpersonal techniques influence actor embodiment, emotional authenticity, and artistic depth. The research situates acting as a phenomenological process, wherein the performer's engagement with role and audience becomes a transformative experience. In doing so, this book contributes to the evolving interdisciplinary dialogue between psychology, performance studies, and consciousness research.

Why This Exploration Matters: Purpose and Significanc

A New Approach to Actor Training

Actors have long sought methods to enhance their craft—not just in terms of technical skill but in the deeper, psychological dimensions of performance. Great acting requires more than mere memorization of lines or physical execution of stage directions; it demands a full embodiment of character, an ability to channel emotions authentically, and a heightened awareness of self and space. Over time, the methodologies used in actor training have expanded, incorporating techniques drawn from psychology, movement, and mindfulness practices.

Yet, despite the growing body of research on acting methodologies, one significan gap remains: how transpersonal psychology—particularly through the practices of aikido and mindfulness meditation—might shape and enhance an actor's psychological depth, emotional flexibilit , and stage presence. While aikido and mindfulness meditation have been widely studied for their cognitive and physiological effects (Chiesa, Calati, & Serretti, 2011; Kabat-Zinn, 2003), their potential to transform the actor's craft through a transpersonal lens has yet to be fully explored.

This book takes up that challenge. By examining how aikido and mindfulness meditation contribute to an actor's psychological preparedness, emotional depth, and ability to inhabit a role, we begin to uncover a new paradigm in actor training—one that integrates mind, body, and consciousness in a deeply profound way.

Acting as a Journey into the Self and Beyond

The craft of acting is, at its core, an exercise in self-exploration and transcendence. The greatest actors are not merely performers; they are individuals who fully dissolve into their roles, creating characters that resonate with truth and emotional depth. This transformation requires not only technical skill but a deep psychological engagement with the nature of selfhood, identity, and emotional fluidit .

Transpersonal psychology, as a discipline, concerns itself with precisely these dimensions of human experience—the ways in which consciousness expands beyond the self, the intersection of identity and transcendence, and the capacity to reach beyond personal limitations into a larger, interconnected awareness (Scotton, 1996). In many ways, acting and transpersonal psychology share a common pursuit: the exploration of self through transformation, the integration of multiple identities, and the pursuit of a reality beyond ordinary experience.

By engaging with aikido and mindfulness meditation, actors are given tools to deepen their self-awareness, cultivate presence, and refine their ability to shift between psychological states with greater ease. These methods offer more than simple relaxation techniques; they provide a structured pathway for actors to develop a heightened sense of emotional intelligence, embodiment, and character immersion.

Through the practice of aikido, actors learn to flow with ene gy rather than resist it, cultivating a sensitivity to movement, breath, and emotional expression that is invaluable on stage. Similarly, mindfulness meditation trains the mind to stay present, observe emotions without attachment, and engage deeply with the moment—qualities that are at the heart of compelling performances.

Uncovering the Psychological and Spiritual Nexus in Performance

Theater is not merely an art form; it is a reflection of human psychology, emotion, and spiritual experience. Every performance, in some way, is an exploration of what it means to be human. Actors, in taking on roles, must navigate a complex interplay of emotions, motivations, and psychological states, stepping beyond their personal identities to embody another's lived experience.

Aikido and mindfulness meditation, both deeply rooted in spiritual and philosophical traditions, provide a fascinating lens through which to explore this process. Their shared emphasis on awareness, energy, and the dissolution of egoic barriers offers a potential bridge between the psychological, spiritual, and performative aspects of acting.

This book seeks to explore:

How aikido and mindfulness meditation influence an actor's ability to regulate emotions, sustain presence, and enter immersive psychological states.

What role embodied spiritual awareness plays in shaping an actor's creative expression and connection to a role.

How transpersonal practices can be harnessed to enhance artistic depth, spontaneity, and resilience in performance.

Through this exploration, we aim to uncover new possibilities for actor training, integrating transpersonal methodologies into the practice of performance in a way that deepens emotional resonance, enhances presence, and refines character embodiment

Beyond Theory: A Practical Framework for Actor Training

While this book engages deeply with theoretical foundations, it is ultimately driven by a practical goal—to offer a tested, evidence-based approach for integrating transpersonal techniques into actor training. Using a structured research methodology, this study:

1.Examines the impact of aikido and mindfulness meditation on an actor's ability to inhabit roles, manage emotions, and maintain psychological resilience on stage.

2. Identifies both the shared and distinct benefits of these transpersonal practices, revealing how they enhance different aspects of acting performance.

3.Develops an integrated training model that actors, directors, and educators can apply to enhance stage presence, deepen character work, and cultivate emotional dexterity.

In essence, this book seeks to demonstrate that acting is not merely a craft of imitation, but a profound psychological and transpersonal endeavor. By bringing together insights from transpersonal psychology, embodied cognition, and performance studies, we aim to redefine the way actors approach their art, their psychology, and their creative potential.

Transforming Theater Through Transpersonal Psychology

From a pedagogical standpoint, this book presents a compelling case for the integration of transpersonal methodologies into performance education. Acting schools and conservatories have long incorporated psychological training into their curricula, but few have systematically explored the potential of transpersonal psychology as a tool for artistic development.

By validating the role of aikido and mindfulness meditation in actor training, this work seeks to:

Expand the discourse on performance psychology, illustrating the ways in which transpersonal awareness enhances an actor's ability to navigate emotional and psychological complexity.

Offer a new model for actor training, integrating both spiritual and psychological development into traditional theatrical methodologies.

Demonstrate that the principles of aikido and mindfulness meditation can cultivate greater authenticity, presence, and expressivity in actors, leading to more powerful and resonant performances.

By bridging the gap between transpersonal psychology and performance studies, this book aims to reshape the way we think about actor training, offering new pathways for artistic and psychological growth.

Unveiling the Central Inquiry

At the intersection of psychology and performance lies an essential question: What inner mechanisms allow actors to embody roles with authenticity, depth, and emotional resonance? Throughout history, actors have employed a myriad of training methodologies—ranging from classical theatrical techniques to contemporary psychological interventions—each designed to deepen their understanding of character and enhance their stage presence. Yet, one dimension of performance training remains largely unexplored: the potential of transpersonal psychological methods to cultivate heightened awareness, emotional fluidit , and psychological resilience in actors.

This book investigates this phenomenon through a central inquiry:

How do transpersonal psychological methodologies—specifically aikido and mindfulness meditation—impact the cognitive, emotional, and embodied processes of acting performance?

To fully examine this question, this study also considers a set of supporting inquiries that account for variations in individual actors' experiences, skill levels, and demographic differences.

Fundamental Questions That Guide This Book

The Core Question

At the heart of this inquiry is the foundational research question:

To what extent do transpersonal psychological methods, including aikido and mindfulness meditation, influence the psychological, cognitive, and performative dimensions of an actor's craft?

This question seeks to evaluate whether these methodologies contribute to emotional regulation, enhance presence, and refine an actor's ability to transition seamlessly between states of consciousness in performance.

Supporting Perspectives

Beyond the primary research question, a deeper investigation is required to discern how transpersonal methodologies interact with individual variables, such as an actor's gender, age, cultural background, and professional experience. This study, therefore, explores four critical sub-questions:

1.Gender and Expressivity – Does the integration of transpersonal psychology influence male and female actors differently? If so, how do these methodologies shape their emotional depth, role immersion, and psychological adaptation on stage?

2.Age and Embodiment – Does the effectiveness of aikido and mindfulness meditation differ based on an actor's age? Are younger actors more receptive to these methodologies, or do experienced performers derive more profound benefits from transpersonal training

3.Cultural Dimensions – How do actors from Eastern and Western traditions respond to transpersonal psychological training? Does prior exposure to meditative or somatic practices influence the efficacy of these methods in performance?

4.Professional Experience and Cognitive Adaptability – How do transpersonal methodologies affect seasoned actors compared to those in the early stages of their training? Do professional actors integrate these techniques differently than novice performers?

By addressing these dimensions, this book aims to articulate a comprehensive framework for understanding the role of transpersonal psychology in actor training, illustrating both its universal applicability and the nuanced ways in which it manifests across different performers.

Approach and Methods: A Roadmap for Discovery

Experimental Design and Methodological Framework

To systematically evaluate the impact of transpersonal psychological methodologies on performance, this study adopts a controlled experimental design, conducted at Sofia University. The research involves both qualitative and quantitative analysis, structured into comparative experimental conditions to examine the effects of aikido and mindfulness meditation on actors' stage performance.

Participants and Study Structure

The study comprises 40 actor-participants and 10 evaluators, selected from a diverse volunteer pool. The three-stage experimental process is outlined as follows:

1.Initial Performance Assessment – Participants perform a brief scripted scene without prior exposure to transpersonal psychological training. Their performances are evaluated by an audience panel using standardized scoring criteria.

2.Transpersonal Training Intervention – Participants undergo a structured regimen of aikido and mindfulness meditation training, designed to enhance somatic awareness, refine emotional regulation, and develop present-moment attentiveness.

3.Post-Training Performance Evaluation – Participants perform a second scripted scene following their training, and their performances are re-evaluated by the same audience panel, allowing for direct comparative analysis of pre- and post-intervention results.

Contrastive Analysis: Investigating Individual Variability

To further explore individual differences in response to transpersonal methodologies, participants were divided into comparative study groups, categorized as follows:

Group 1: Professional vs. Non-Professional Actors – Assessing whether trained actors incorporate transpersonal training differently than novices.

Group 2: Gender-Based Comparisons – Investigating whether male and female actors exhibit distinct responses to transpersonal methodologies in performance.

Group 3: Cultural Influence – Analyzing differences between actors from Eastern traditions (e.g., China, Japan) and Western traditions (e.g., the United States, Europe) in response to these practices.

Group 4: Age-Based Analysis – Comparing the effects of transpersonal training on younger actors (ages 20-35) versus more experienced actors (ages 35-50).

By utilizing this contrastive methodology, the study seeks to identify both the overarching impact of transpersonal psychological training and the subtle ways in which individual characteristics influence its effectiveness.

Navigating the Chapters Ahead

This book unfolds across five core chapters, each structured to build a progressive, multidimensional understanding of transpersonal psychology's role in performance training.

Chapter 1: Establishing the Inquiry

The opening chapter introduces the foundational research questions, situating them within the broader discourse of transpersonal psychology and performance studies. It outlines the theoretical significance, research design, and key inquiries guiding this work.

Chapter 2: Theoretical Foundations and Literature Review

The second chapter explores the historical and theoretical landscape of transpersonal psychology, detailing its evolution and relevance to the psychology of acting. It critically reviews existing research on embodiment, consciousness, and the psychological dimensions of performance, positioning aikido and mindfulness meditation within this broader scholarly context.

Chapter 3: Methodology and Research Design

Chapter 3 provides an in-depth analysis of the experimental structure, participant selection, training interventions, and assessment techniques used in this study. It explains the rationale behind the contrastive study design, ensuring methodological transparency and academic rigor.

Chapter 4: Empirical Findings and Performance Analysis

The fourth chapter presents the data collected from the experimental study, highlighting observable changes in stage presence, emotional adaptability, and cognitive engagement after transpersonal training. It offers a detailed analysis of statistical outcomes, participant refle - tions, and audience evaluations.

Chapter 5: Implications, Challenges, and Future Directions

The final chapter synthesizes the findings within a broader theoretical and practical framework, discussing the implications for acting training, performance psychology, and transpersonal research. It also outlines limitations of the study and potential areas for future inquiry.

Appendices

This book is supplemented by an extensive appendix section, which includes:

Performance Evaluation Forms – Used for audience assessment of actors' performances.

Experimental Scripts – The dramatic texts used in pre- and post-training performance evaluations.

Survey Instruments – Questionnaires designed to gauge actors' subjective experiences with transpersonal psychological training.

Chapter 2

Foundations of Thought and Practice

A Landscape of Ideas: Situating This Book in the Broader Dialogue

Every profound intellectual journey begins with a conversation—a convergence of ideas, perspectives, and insights that shape our understanding of the world. This chapter serves as an invitation to such a dialogue, guiding us into the realm of transpersonal psychology, a discipline that merges scientific inquiry with contemplative traditions to explore the nature of transformation, creativity, and performance.

This chapter unfolds in two parts. The first section focuses on the empirical literature review, tracing how past research has examined the real-world applications of transpersonal psychology. How do practices such as aikido and mindfulness meditation influence human experience? Do they truly enhance performance, deepen self-awareness, and alter states of consciousness? Rather than merely summarizing prior studies, this section seeks to uncover underlying patterns, weaving together disparate research findings to present a coherent and evolving picture of transpersonal psychology's practical dimensions.

However, data alone cannot tell the full story. To grasp the true scope of transpersonal psychology, we must also explore the conceptual frameworks that support it. The second section delves into the theoretical literature review, analyzing key theories, dominant models, and foundational philosophical debates that have shaped transpersonal psychology. What does it mean to transcend the self? How do transpersonal states intersect with creative and performative expression? This section examines the convergence of ancient wisdom traditions and contemporary psychological thought, demonstrating how aikido and mindfulness meditation function not just as techniques but as gateways to profound cognitive and emotional transformation. Furthermore, it explores how these practices inform acting theories, embodied cognition, and artistic development, shedding light on the deeper interplay between psychology and performance.

Yet, this chapter is more than an academic survey—it is an intellectual journey through a landscape of ideas, where psychology meets spirituality, where scientific inquiry intersects with intuition, and where the boundaries between self and transcendence, performer and performance, thought and experience begin to dissolve. By weaving together empirical insights with theoretical depth, this chapter aims to engage the reader in a living, evolving dialogue, one that extends beyond passive reading into active exploration. Here, transpersonal psychology is not presented as a fixed body of knowledge but as a dynamic and expanding field—one that continues to redefine itself, inviting us to question, discover, and participate in its unfolding story.

Empirical Perspectives on Transpersonal Psychology-- Origins and Evolution of Transpersonal Thought

The term transpersonal psychology was first introduced by William James in a 1905 lecture. However, at the time, it remained a descriptive phrase rather than a systematically developed concept. In 1917, Carl

Jung introduced the German term überpersönlich to describe states of consciousness beyond the individual self, which was later translated into English. Despite these early conceptualizations, transpersonal psychology did not emerge as an independent discipline until the 1960s, when it developed as an extension of humanistic psychology (Sutich, 1972). Abraham Maslow and Anthony Sutich were among the central figures shaping this field. Sutich, deeply influence by mysticism and both Eastern and Western philosophical traditions, explored Hindu Vedas, Buddhist philosophy, and Christian theology. Similarly, Maslow's later work incorporated Eastern perspectives, providing a theoretical foundation for transpersonal psychology.

Transpersonal psychology arose at the intersection of Eastern and Western intellectual traditions. From the 1960s onward, psychologists increasingly engaged with non-Western perspectives, incorporating insights from Confucian, Taoist, Buddhist, and Indian psychological frameworks. A central realization emerged: despite cultural differences, both Eastern and Western traditions acknowledged a transpersonal dimension—one that extends beyond the individual self. Tu (1985) argued that Confucian philosophy inherently involves a dynamic spiritual process, suggesting that the self is simultaneously sacred and transcendent, originating from destiny and fundamentally interconnected with the cosmos. This perspective aligns with transpersonal psychology's emphasis on self-transcendence as a fundamental psychological drive. Similarly, Assagioli (1974) developed the framework of psychosynthesis, distinguishing transpersonal psychology from other psychological models by asserting the reality of spirituality and higher states of consciousness.

Bridging Eastern and Western Thought in Transpersonal Psychology

Transpersonal psychology not only emerged as a distinct school of thought but also served as an intellectual bridge between Eastern and Western traditions (Taylor, 1992). This integration fostered an interdisciplinary dialogue, with scholars such as Ken Wilber (1993) categorizing knowledge in psychology into sensorial, intellectual, and contemplative dimensions. Wilber argued that only knowledge derived from sensory experience could be classified as scientific in the conventional sense. However, transpersonal psychology extends beyond the empirical focus of mainstream Western psychology, integrating the contemplative wisdom of Eastern traditions, particularly Buddhist concepts of emptiness and ego dissolution (Maslow, 1976).

A defining characteristic of transpersonal psychology is its recognition of spirituality as an essential component of human experience. While mainstream Western psychology has historically marginalized spirituality, transpersonal psychology regards it as central to psychological well-being. Geisler (1983) criticized materialist reductionism, which denies the transpersonal realm, arguing that strict adherence to physicalist paradigms limits our understanding of human consciousness. Similarly, Einstein (1979) suggested that true scientific inquiry must acknowledge the existence of spiritual dimensions within the universe. Eddington (1984) extended this argument, noting that while the physical sciences excel in empirical precision, they remain insufficient for comprehending the phenomena beyond the observable world.

Methodological Approaches in Transpersonal Psychology

The methodological foundations of transpersonal psychology differ significantly from those of traditional psychological research. Early mainstream psychologists sought to apply the empirical methodologies of physics to psychology, aiming to establish it as an objective science. As a result, many rejected spirituality as an area of serious inquiry. However, some physicists, including Heisenberg (1965), critiqued the rigidity of this approach, arguing that scientific paradigms had become overly mechanistic and inflexible. The dominance of materialist models led to a neglect of fundamental psychological constructs, such as consciousness, the psyche, and subjective experience. Frank (1975) warned that rejecting self-transcendence diminishes psychology's capacity to explore the deeper meaning and value of human existence. Similarly, Tart (1977) observed that mainstream Western psychology's exclusion of spirituality contributed to existential distress and emotional disconnection in contemporary society.

Despite initial resistance, transpersonal psychology persisted due to the efforts of pioneering scholars. Progoff (1973) contended that psychology loses its fundamental purpose if it fails to acknowledge human spirituality. Alfred Adler called for renewed attention to spirituality in psychology, seeing it as integral to personal growth and self-actualization. Rank (1950) further challenged Freud's reductionist view of the self, arguing that true selfhood is rooted in both ancestral and collective spiritual dimensions, rather than being confined to personal history.

The Establishment of Transpersonal Psychology as the "Fourth Force"

Following behaviorism (the "first force"), psychoanalysis (the "second force"), and humanistic psychology (the "third force"), transpersonal psychology emerged as the "fourth force" in psychology (Sutich, 1968). By the mid-1960s, Maslow and Sutich had become increasingly dissatisfied with the limitations of humanistic psychology, particularly its focus on self-actualization without addressing transcendent experiences. Maslow (1976) argued that psychology must address existential and spiritual dimensions to contribute meaningfully to human development. He criticized traditional psychology for its fragmented understanding of personality, asserting that a holistic model must incorporate both personal and transpersonal dimensions.

Roberto Assagioli made significant contributions to transpersonal psychology through his theory of psychosynthesis, which he divided into two developmental stages. The first stage involves achieving self-integration, balance, and psychological control, while the second focuses on the psychosynthesis of spirit, in which the self develops through interactions with the transpersonal realm. Scotton (1996) identified the superconscious as the source of transpersonal experiences, suggesting that these states can be cultivated through meditation, guided imagery, and other contemplative practices.

Transpersonal psychologists have developed comprehensive theoretical models to describe the structure of consciousness. Wilber (1993) proposed the spectrum of consciousness model, while Tart (1993) introduced a systemic view of consciousness, both of which highlight the multidimensional nature of human awareness. Taylor (1992) emphasized that transpersonal psychology bridges psychoanalysis and humanistic psychology, offering a framework that integrates depth psychology with higher states of consciousness.

Key Approaches and Transformational Practices

The methods of transpersonal psychology are rooted in its theoretical aim of exploring the fundamental nature of human consciousness, potential, and transcendence. This field seeks to integrate the spiritual traditions of various cultures with modern psychological perspectives, fostering an approach that combines creativity with an understanding of the "body-mind-spirit" connection. By doing so, transpersonal psychology offers a holistic framework for comprehending the human experience. Drawing from its foundation in humanistic psychology, transpersonal psychology has been shaped by both Eastern and Western thought, incorporating insights from Buddhism, classical Chinese psychology, Taoist breathing techniques, and the meditative and yogic traditions of India. Its overarching goal is to examine human potential, the search for truth, and the dynamics of self-transcendence as a means of facilitating the soul's development.

Li (1997) synthesized transpersonal psychology's core concerns into three fundamental propositions. First, beyond physiological and psychological dimensions, the spiritual aspect of human existence must also be considered. This perspective recognizes that the human experience extends beyond cognitive and behavioral processes to include deeper existential and transcendental elements. Second, transpersonal psychology challenges the traditional understanding of the "self," asserting that individuals often become overly identified with their personal identities, self-concepts, and ego structures. However, what one perceives as the "self" may not be an accurate representation of one's true nature or "real self." Finally, transpersonal psychology posits that true personal growth involves transcending the ego-bound self. Humans are not isolated entities but part of a larger interconnected reality. Understanding and engaging in transpersonal processes allows individuals to move beyond their limited sense of self, ultimately fostering self-transcendence and the realization of a more authentic existence.

In terms of methodology, transpersonal psychology advocates for diverse and flexible research approaches that align with its broad and integrative perspective. Given its emphasis on subjective experience, altered states of consciousness, and personal transformation, the field has traditionally relied on qualitative methods, including laboratory and natural experiments, case studies, and phenomenological inquiry. Taylor (1992) emphasized the value of qualitative research in transpersonal psychology, arguing that its strength lies in its ability to capture the richness and depth of human experience (Harari, 1981). However, while qualitative methodologies are widely favored, transpersonal psychology does not disregard empirical rigor. Leahey (1981) noted that researchers in this field can adhere to scientific principles while remaining open to the complexities of spiritual and transcendent phenomena. The challenge lies in balancing systematic inquiry with the inherently subjective nature of transpersonal experiences.

Various methodological approaches have been utilized in transpersonal psychology research, each serving different aspects of human experience. From a physiological perspective, movement-based practices such as dance, outdoor activities, and yoga have been employed to explore the relationship between physical embodiment and altered states of consciousness. In studies focusing on consciousness and awareness, meditation and mindfulness practices have been extensively examined for their effects on self-perception, cognitive processes, and well-being. Additionally, techniques such as guided imagery, instructional fantasy, and autohypnosis have been used to investigate creative inspiration and deep introspection, offering insight into how individuals access and navigate transpersonal states.

This study incorporates aikido—a Japanese martial art that embodies principles of harmony, flo , and non-resistance—and mindfulness meditation as methodological tools within transpersonal psychology. Aikido, beyond being a physical discipline, is deeply rooted in the philosophy of blending with external forces rather than resisting them, making it a compelling metaphor for the integration of self and other. Mindfulness meditation, by contrast, serves as a structured contemplative practice that cultivates present-moment awareness and facilitates the dissolution of egoic boundaries. By integrating these approaches, this research seeks to provide empirical insights into how transpersonal psychological methods can be applied in real-world settings. Specificall , it examines how such methods may contribute to performance-related disciplines, offering potential pathways for individuals to overcome personal limitations, deepen their presence, and access heightened states of creative engagement.

Ultimately, transpersonal psychology's methodological landscape reflects its broader philosophical orientation: an openness to diverse approaches, a commitment to experiential depth, and a recognition of the intricate interplay between the personal and the transcendent. This dynamic and integrative perspective positions transpersonal psychology as a field uniquely suited to exploring the profound and often ineffable dimensions of human existence.

Transpersonal Psychology as a Tool for Artistic Growth

The application of transpersonal psychology extends far beyond theoretical discourse, permeating various domains of human experience where the cultivation of self-awareness, spirituality, and expanded consciousness plays a transformative role. At its core, transpersonal psychology offers a pathway for individuals to engage with deeper layers of existence, fostering an understanding of the self that transcends conventional psychological frameworks. It is not merely a discipline concerned with cognition or behavior but one that integrates embodied practice, spiritual insight, and creative exploration. Prior research has illuminated its capacity to nurture personal transformation, revealing its impact on self-development, emotional regulation, and the cultivation of meaning. It has been employed in therapeutic settings, meditative disciplines, and creative endeavors, each of which underscores its function as both a psychological inquiry and a lived practice.

Within this broader landscape, this study examines transpersonal psychology not as an isolated academic field but as an experiential process interwoven with the realm of dramatic performance. The performative act—whether on stage or in daily life—is a dynamic expression of human consciousness. Actors, in their pursuit of authenticity, presence, and emotional depth, must cultivate a heightened sensitivity to the body-mind connection. The act of stepping into a role necessitates a form of self-transcendence, in which the boundaries of the individual ego dissolve, giving way to a more expansive awareness. It is in this liminal space—between self and character, between embodied presence and imaginative immersion—that transpersonal psychology finds its application. By incorporating transpersonal methods into performance training, actors are afforded tools to deepen their engagement with their craft, transforming their artistic expression into a process of both personal and collective transcendence.

This study introduces two transpersonal psychological training methods—Aikido and mindfulness meditation—as key components in performance training. Aikido, a martial art rooted in Japanese spiritual philosophy, emphasizes harmony, fluidit , and the dissolution of resistance. It trains practitioners to move with, rather than against, external forces, cultivating a heightened somatic awareness that is invaluable to actors seeking to refine their physical expressiveness. Mindfulness meditation, on the other hand, fosters a disciplined yet expansive state of awareness, allowing actors to cultivate attentional control, emotional receptivity, and an immersive presence in their roles. While Aikido provides a kinetic pathway into transpersonal embodiment, mindfulness meditation grounds the actor in the immediacy of experience, facilitating a state of being fully attuned to the moment. Together, these practices serve as bridges between psychological introspection and performative enactment, offering a holistic approach to training that transcends conventional acting techniques.

The existing body of research on transpersonal psychology can be broadly categorized into three key domains. The first pertains to its theoretical underpinnings, encompassing its philosophical foundations, historical evolution, and conceptual framework. This domain explores the epistemological breadth of transpersonal psychology, situating it within the broader discourse of psychology, spirituality, and human development. The second domain focuses on the practical effects of transpersonal psychology, synthesizing empirical findings on its impact on cognitive flexibilit , emotional regulation, and self-actualization. This body of research has demonstrated its efficacy in fostering resilience, creativity, and heightened states of consciousness. The third domain examines its therapeutic applications, an area that has gained increasing recognition within both clinical and non-clinical settings. Transpersonal interventions have been implemented in psychotherapeutic contexts, meditative traditions, and expressive arts therapies, underscoring their capacity to facilitate healing and transformation.

This study contributes to the existing literature by foregrounding the application of transpersonal methods within the performative arts. While previous research has largely centered on either theoretical constructs or therapeutic interventions, this study positions transpersonal psychology within the embodied and creative practice of performance. By integrating transpersonal techniques into actor training, it seeks to offer a new perspective on how performers can access deeper layers of presence, authenticity, and creative flo . Performance, in this view, becomes more than an artistic endeavor—it emerges as a transpersonal experience, a site of transformation in which self and other, performer and audience, converge in a shared moment of transcendence. Through this integration, the study not only expands the practical applications of transpersonal psychology but also illuminates its potential as a vehicle for artistic and personal evolution.

Performance and Transpersonal Awareness: A Theoretical Connection

Acting is far more than a technical skill; it is a deeply psychological and often transformative experience that requires the performer to navigate between self and character, between reality and illusion. Throughout history, actors have described moments of complete immersion in a role—states in which the boundaries between their own identity and the character they portray seem to dissolve. This phenomenon, often described as "flow" in contemporary psychology, resonates strongly with the concept of self-transcendence in transpersonal psychology. While previous research has acknowledged the altered states of consciousness that actors experience during performance, few studies have examined this phenomenon through a transpersonal lens. Even fewer have provided structured training methods that harness the principles of transpersonal psychology to support an actor's artistic and psychological development.

The process of performance involves not only embodying a role but also engaging in continuous self-exploration. Each character an actor plays presents a new challenge, a new psychological terrain to navigate, requiring them to move beyond their habitual self-concept. In this sense, acting can be understood as a practice of transformation— one that extends beyond mere imitation and into the realm of deep personal and artistic discovery. However, this process is not without conflict. Actors often experience tension between their personal identity and the characters they portray, a phenomenon commonly referred to as "role conflict." In traditional acting methodologies, performers are encouraged to analyze and inhabit a character through external techniques such as physical gestures, vocal modulation, and script analysis. While these methods are effective, they often overlook the deeper psychological and spiritual dimensions of performance. Transpersonal psychology, by contrast, offers a framework for navigating these conflicts in a way that integrates mind, body, and spirit. Rather than merely adopting a role, an actor can learn to become the role—not through forced identification but through a process of conscious transcendence, where the actor merges elements of self and character into a unified artistic expression

Incorporating transpersonal psychology into performance training introduces a new perspective on how actors engage with their craft. This study explores the potential of Aikido and mindfulness meditation as transpersonal training methods for performers. Aikido, a Japanese martial art founded on principles of harmony and non-resistance, is not just a physical discipline but also a philosophy of movement and flo . It teaches practitioners to blend with external forces rather than resist them—a concept that holds profound relevance for actors who must surrender to the energy of a scene while maintaining presence and control. Aikido's emphasis on balance, adaptation, and fluidity mirrors the mental and emotional agility required in acting, making it a compelling practice for those seeking to refine their performance skills

Mindfulness meditation, on the other hand, cultivates a heightened state of awareness that allows actors to fully inhabit the present moment. One of the greatest challenges in performance is maintaining authenticity under the pressures of scripted dialogue, stage directions, and audience expectations. Mindfulness training enhances an actor's ability to remain fully engaged with their emotions and physical presence without becoming overwhelmed or disconnected. Through mindfulness, performers learn to observe their thoughts and feelings without attachment, enabling them to channel emotions in a way that serves the character rather than being hindered by personal psychological barriers. Both Aikido and mindfulness, when integrated into actor training, offer a structured yet fluid approach to self-transcendence— one that allows performers to access deeper layers of expression and artistic truth.

Previous studies on performance psychology have typically been divided into three main areas: theoretical discussions on the nature of acting and self-transcendence, empirical studies on the effects of psychological states in performance, and therapeutic applications of drama, such as psychodrama and drama therapy. While these fields have contributed valuable insights, they have largely treated transpersonal states as incidental rather than integral to the craft of acting. This research seeks to bridge this gap by providing empirical evidence of transpersonal processes in actor training. By employing controlled contrast experiments, it examines how transpersonal methods infl - ence performance outcomes, shedding light on the ways in which actors can consciously cultivate altered states of awareness to enhance their artistic capabilities.

In addition to deepening our understanding of performance psychology, this study also revisits the fundamental triad of performance: the actor, the role, and the audience. Traditional research has explored these three components in isolation, yet few studies have analyzed their interconnection from a transpersonal perspective. Performance is not a static process; it is an exchange of energy, an interaction that extends beyond the individual. When an actor fully embodies a role, they become a conduit for something greater than themselves—a story, an emotion, an archetype that transcends personal identity. The audience, in turn, becomes part of this shared experience, engaging in an un-spoken dialogue that exists beyond words. Transpersonal psychology offers a model for understanding this phenomenon, suggesting that the most compelling performances arise not when an actor "performs" a role but when they surrender to it, allowing themselves to become a vessel for artistic and psychological transformation.

This study ultimately proposes a new paradigm for actor training—one grounded in the transpersonal framework of body-mind-spirit. In contrast to conventional acting methods that emphasize external tech-nique, this approach prioritizes internal transformation, encouraging actors to explore their own consciousness as a means of deepening their artistic practice. It suggests that the most powerful performances emerge not through force or imitation but through presence, fluidit , and self-transcendence. Just as a masterful musician does not merely play notes but inhabits the music, a truly great actor does not simply portray a character but becomes an instrument through which the char-acter is expressed.

By integrating transpersonal methods into actor training, this study offers a pathway not only for improved performance but also for per-sonal growth. The process of acting becomes more than an artistic endeavor; it becomes a means of self-discovery, a practice through which performers can explore the depths of their own being. In this light, transpersonal psychology is not simply a tool for refining tech-nique—it is a philosophy of engagement, an invitation for actors to transcend the limitations of self and step into the boundless possibilities of human expression.

The Role of Aikido and Mindfulness in Actor Development

Aikido and mindfulness meditation, though originating from different traditions, share a profound connection in their emphasis on harmonizing internal and external forces. Both practices cultivate self-awareness, discipline, and a heightened state of presence, which are crucial in stage performance training. This section examines Aikido and mindfulness meditation from their individual perspectives and explores their combined impact on actor training. While previous studies have assessed these practices separately, few have analyzed their training effects through the lens of transpersonal psychology. This research aims to bridge that gap by demonstrating how these disciplines contribute to the cognitive, emotional, and physical dimensions of performance.

Aikido is a comprehensive martial art that integrates throwing, joint-locking, and striking techniques. Unlike conventional combat sports that focus on overpowering an opponent, Aikido emphasizes balance, fluidit , and non-resistance. Practitioners do not seek to defeat their opponents but rather to blend with their movements, redirecting force rather than opposing it directly. Traditionally, Aikido practitioners train with Japanese weapons such as the bokken (wooden sword) and tanto (knife) to refine their technique. However, these weapons are not viewed as instruments of violence but as tools for cultivating coordination, focus, and inner harmony. The aim of Aikido is not combat but rather the cooperative development of physical and psychological resilience through controlled movement.

Founded by Morihei Ueshiba in the early 20th century, Aikido was influenced by various Eastern martial arts, particularly those from China and India. Ueshiba envisioned Aikido as a non-competitive discipline that sought to integrate the practitioner with the natural order of existence. In this sense, Aikido training is not merely about physical defense but also about fostering a deeper connection between mind, body, and environment. The philosophy of Aikido extends beyond technical movements to encompass broader spiritual principles, including the idea of universal peace and reconciliation. Ueshiba believed that true martial mastery was not about defeating others but about achieving self-mastery through internal balance. The combat in Aikido is, therefore, metaphorical—a process of engaging with opposing forces and resolving tension through movement rather than resistance.

Aikido also embodies the principle of counterbalance, in which practitioners use an opponent's strength to their advantage rather than meeting force with force. This principle is not only relevant in self-defense but also in psychological and emotional regulation. Aikido has been studied for its effects on cognitive and emotional stability, with research suggesting that it fosters self-awareness, emotional regulation, and interpersonal harmony (Rudisill, 2007). Unlike other martial arts that focus on aggression, Aikido emphasizes harmony in conflict resolution, making it an ideal practice for actors who must navigate the emotional intensity of performance while maintaining psychological equilibrium. The interplay between movement and mindfulness in Aikido reflects the same principles that actors rely on in their craft—fluid adaptation, heightened awareness, and the ability to remain present in the moment.

The spiritual and psychological benefits of Aikido have been wide-ly studied. Faggianelli (2006) argued that Aikido fosters a state of self-transcendence, enabling practitioners to shift from a reactive mindset to one of intentional presence. Dykhuizen (2000) noted that the essence of Aikido lies in creating harmony rather than engaging in physical confrontation, reinforcing the idea that the martial art is as much about internal balance as it is about external movement. Similar-ly, Ueshiba himself maintained that aggression and violence could be neutralized through the harmonious coordination of spirit and move-ment. Ernest (1991) documented the case of Thomas, a man who had suffered childhood trauma and found relief through Aikido training. After practicing Aikido, Thomas experienced a profound transforma-tion, reporting reduced aggression, increased energy, and a renewed sense of psychological stability. These findings suggest that Aikido training can be applied beyond the realm of self-defense, offering po-tential therapeutic benefits in conflict resolution, mediation, and per-sonal development.

Mindfulness meditation, though distinct from Aikido in practice, shares a similar goal of cultivating presence and inner harmony. Root-ed in Buddhist and Hindu traditions, mindfulness meditation has been recognized for its psychological and physiological benefits, including stress reduction, enhanced cognitive function, and improved emotion-al regulation (Harris, Jennings, Katz, Abenavoli, & Greenberg, 2016; Keng, Smoski, & Robins, 2016). Unlike Aikido, which involves dy-namic physical movement, mindfulness meditation is a practice of stillness, requiring practitioners to focus their attention on the breath, bodily sensations, or present-moment awareness.

Mindfulness meditation involves a process of continuous redirection of attention. Practitioners are encouraged to sit in an upright posture, focus on their breathing, and observe their thoughts without attachment. Kabat-Zinn (1990) described mindfulness as a tool for disengaging from habitual cognitive patterns, allowing individuals to cultivate a heightened state of awareness. This practice has been linked to improvements in executive function, attentional control, and emotional resilience (Slagter, Davidson, & Lutz, 2011). For actors, mindfulness training can be particularly beneficial in managing stage anxiety, improving concentration, and fostering a deeper connection with their roles. Studies have shown that mindfulness practice enhances an individual's ability to maintain presence in high-pressure situations, a skill that is essential in performance training (Duke, Sperling, & Kapsali, 2016).

One of the most significant applications of mindfulness meditation in performance training is its ability to regulate emotional states. Kristeller and Rikhye (2008) suggested that mindfulness allows individuals to break free from cycles of rumination and self-doubt, enabling them to approach performance with greater confidence and ease. Slagter, Davidson, and Lutz (2011) further argued that mindfulness supports three core regulatory skills: monitoring distractions, disengaging from negative thought patterns, and redirecting attention. These abilities are particularly relevant to actors, who must balance technical precision with emotional spontaneity.

The integration of Aikido and mindfulness meditation in actor training offers a novel approach to performance psychology. While Aikido emphasizes movement and external engagement, mindfulness meditation cultivates internal stillness and focused awareness. Both practices, however, facilitate self-transcendence—a crucial aspect of both transpersonal psychology and performance training. Previous studies have examined these disciplines separately, yet few have explored their combined potential. This study seeks to bridge that gap by investigating how Aikido and mindfulness meditation can be applied together to enhance an actor's ability to achieve presence, adaptability, and artistic depth.

The Living Theater, an experimental theater company, was among the first to incorporate Eastern practices such as yoga and Tai Chi into actor training, recognizing the value of these disciplines in fostering embodied awareness and expressive freedom (Kapsali, 2013). The integration of Aikido and mindfulness meditation follows a similar trajectory, offering a holistic approach to training that aligns with the transpersonal model of body-mind-spirit integration. Hodge (2000) argued that a fundamental principle underlying actor training is "co-or-dination"—the ability to integrate inner experience with external expression. This principle is reflected in both Aikido and mindfulness, making them valuable tools for actors seeking to refine their craft

From a broader perspective, performance itself can be understood as a form of self-transcendence. The ability to step beyond personal identity and embody another character requires a dissolution of ego and a willingness to surrender to the present moment. Aikido teaches practitioners to move with energy rather than against it, much like an actor must adapt to the flow of a performance. Mindfulness meditation cultivates the ability to remain fully engaged without attachment, a skill that is equally crucial in acting. Together, these disciplines offer a comprehensive framework for training that goes beyond technical skill, addressing the psychological and spiritual dimensions of performance.

This research contributes to the growing body of literature on transpersonal psychology and performance training by examining how Aikido and mindfulness meditation can be applied to actor development. By integrating these practices, actors may gain new insights into their craft, developing not only greater technical proficiency but also a deeper sense of artistic and personal authenticity. Performance, in this context, is not merely an external display but a transformative process—one that mirrors the broader journey of self-discovery and transcendence.

The practice of transpersonal psychology in actor training presents a unique intersection of psychology, philosophy, and artistic expression. Unlike early psychological research, which was heavily influenced by natural sciences and relied primarily on experimental methods, transpersonal psychology embraces a broader range of experiential techniques. Early psychologists sought to understand human cognition and behavior through controlled laboratory experiments, but by the mid-20th century, it became evident that such methods had limitations, particularly when applied to the complexities of subjective experience, creativity, and self-transcendence. As a response, researchers began incorporating correlational methods, and under the influence of humanistic psychology—especially existentialism and phenomenology—a more flexible, experience-based approach emerged in the 1960s. This shift aligned seamlessly with the principles of transpersonal psychology, which prioritizes direct personal experience as a pathway to understanding higher states of consciousness.

Jim Vargiu introduced an observational method designed to cultivate heightened awareness. In his approach, participants were instructed to sit in a relaxed environment and engage in detailed observation of their surroundings. This included noting the size, color, and shape of objects while contemplating existential questions such as: Who is see-ing? Who is observing? Who is paying attention to the objects? This exercise was not merely about visual perception but aimed to trigger a deeper awareness of the act of perceiving itself.

To deepen the experiential engagement, participants were also given everyday objects—such as a pen or a book—to hold and explore with their fingers. They were instructed to close their eyes and discern the object's dimensions, texture, and weight purely through touch. This practice was not just a sensory exercise but a way to develop an acute awareness of the distinction between the perceiver and the perceived. By guiding participants to simultaneously acknowledge both the ob-ject and the awareness that perceives it, the exercise fostered a direct encounter with the nature of consciousness.

Roberto Assagioli (1975), a pioneer of transpersonal psychology, en-visioned a "higher psychology program" that would explore the true self—its attributes, capacities, and methods of accessing and utilizing its deeper wisdom. He developed the techniques of non-identification and self-identification as means of experiential engagement with tran-spersonal states. Participants were instructed to sit comfortably, close their eyes, and focus on their breath. This preliminary relaxation pre-pared them to enter a more profound state of awareness. They would then open their eyes and read carefully selected passages related to transpersonal psychology, immersing themselves in the concepts while observing their internal responses. Through repeated practice, individuals could gradually experience a sense of the "real-self"—a dimension of identity beyond the conditioned ego.

At the core of Assagioli's framework is the idea that the human mind operates on multiple levels, with the highest being the domain of the higher subconscious. This level is associated with advanced cognitive and creative capacities, as well as profound experiences of truth, beauty, and ethical insight. While different individuals manifest these qualities in varying degrees, they all have access to this level of consciousness. Throughout history, this phenomenon has been acknowledged across cultures, with different traditions assigning various names to it—whether as divine inspiration, artistic genius, or enlightenment. Despite terminological differences, there is a shared recognition across both Eastern and Western traditions that human beings possess an inner dimension capable of extraordinary perception and creativity.

The concept of the higher self plays a central role in transpersonal psychology. It is a synthesis of individuality and universality, transcending personal identity while still maintaining an individualized expression. Often referred to as the transpersonal self, this aspect of consciousness serves as a bridge between the personal and the universal, allowing individuals to integrate their experiences with a larger collective reality (Brown, 1983, p. 35). This perspective is particularly relevant for actors, as the art of performance requires an ongoing negotiation between personal identity and the embodiment of other characters. When an actor fully immerses themselves in a role, they engage in a process that mirrors the fundamental principles of transpersonal psychology:

stepping beyond the ego, merging with a larger creative force, and accessing a state of presence that transcends ordinary consciousness.

From an artistic standpoint, actors often describe peak performance as a state of flo , in which they feel completely absorbed in their role, unselfconsciously responding to the nuances of the scene with a heightened sense of spontaneity and authenticity. This state resembles the descriptions of self-transcendence found in mystical traditions and transpersonal psychology. The notion that the self is fluid, expansive, and capable of merging with something greater is a recurring theme in both artistic expression and spiritual experience.

In transpersonal psychology, the real self is not limited to an isolated individual identity but is an expression of a greater whole. It is the medium through which individuals connect with others and with the universe itself. For an actor, this translates into the ability to dissolve personal barriers and embody the essence of a character with depth and truth. Great performances often emerge when actors are able to move beyond technical precision and enter a space of deep resonance with the emotions and realities they are portraying.

The implications of transpersonal psychology for actor training are profound. Traditional acting methods emphasize physical technique, emotional recall, and psychological realism, but integrating transpersonal approaches introduces an additional dimension—one that fosters a more holistic connection between mind, body, and spirit. When actors engage in practices that cultivate heightened awareness, such as Vargiu's observational techniques or Assagioli's self-identification exercises, they develop an expanded sense of presence that enhances their performance. They learn not only to embody characters but to navigate the subtle interplay between self and role, between individual experience and collective expression.

Moreover, transpersonal techniques offer a way to address common challenges faced by actors, such as performance anxiety, creative blockages, and difficulties in emotional regulation. By engaging with mindfulness-based practices, actors can develop greater resilience, learning to remain present and centered even in high-pressure situations. Similarly, the exploration of self-transcendence can provide a sense of meaning and artistic fulfillment, helping actors move beyond the mechanistic execution of technique to a deeper engagement with their craft.

Throughout history, artistic and spiritual traditions have overlapped in their recognition of the transformative power of creative expression. The practice of transpersonal psychology in actor training is an extension of this lineage, offering a framework through which performers can explore the nature of self, consciousness, and human connection. In this sense, acting becomes more than just an artistic endeavor—it becomes a process of self-discovery, an ongoing engagement with the fundamental questions of existence.

By integrating transpersonal psychology into actor training, this study seeks to illuminate the deeper psychological and spiritual dimensions of performance. Rather than viewing acting as mere role-playing, this perspective positions it as a means of exploring the vast potential of human consciousness. The ultimate goal is not only to enhance technical skill but to cultivate an approach to acting that is both transformative and transcendent—one that aligns with the timeless pursuit of truth, beauty, and the exploration of the real self.

Theoretical Perspectives: Expanding the Discourse

Defining Transpersonal Psychology Through an Artistic Lens

Transpersonal psychology, at its core, challenges the conventional boundaries of human consciousness by seeking to understand experiences that extend beyond the individual self. The term transpersonal, in its literal sense, means "beyond the self," yet its implications reach far deeper. As Sutich (1968) described, it encompasses a dimension in which personal identity extends beyond the individual to embrace broader aspects of human existence, including collective consciousness, spiritual awareness, and the vast, often uncharted territories of the psyche and cosmos. This perspective represents an evolution of humanistic psychology, pushing its foundational ideas to their furthest limits, seeking breakthroughs where traditional theories meet their conceptual thresholds.

Humanistic psychology had already revolutionized the field by shifting attention from pathology to human potential, yet it remained constrained in its scope. Transpersonal psychology emerged to address this limitation, emphasizing higher states of psychological development and expanding the methodological approaches available to researchers. It sought to go beyond personal fulfillment and self-actualization, venturing into experiences of transcendence, interconnectedness, and what some traditions have referred to as the higher or universal self. By doing so, transpersonal psychology provided a bridge between psychology and spirituality, offering a framework that integrated empirical research with experiential insights drawn from meditation, altered states of consciousness, and mystical experiences.

In conceptualizing the evolution of human consciousness, Walsh and Vaughan (1996) proposed a model that divides the mind into three primary stages: the ex-personal (pre-egoic, instinctual consciousness), the personal (self-aware, ego-based consciousness), and the transpersonal (expansive, integrative consciousness). This continuum suggests that human development is not merely a linear progression but a spectrum of awareness, in which each stage builds upon the previous one. Wilber (2000) emphasized that the human being is a complex integration of body, mind, soul, and spirit, rejecting reductionist models that view these aspects in isolation. Rather than being separate categories, these dimensions exist as a continuous, interwoven reality, much like the color gradations in a spectrum (Scotton, 1996). This conceptual breakthrough allowed transpersonal psychology to offer a more holistic cognitive model, one that redefined traditional psychology by integrating a broader understanding of selfhood and human potential.

One of the most significant theoretical foundations for transpersonal psychology can be traced back to Abraham Maslow's hierarchy of needs. Maslow's contribution extended beyond the conventional psychological understanding of motivation by identifying a distinct, transcendent quality in human development. It was Maslow who first introduced the term trans-humanistic psychology to Sutich, suggesting a new domain that extended beyond self-actualization to what he called self-transcendence (Battista, 1996). His well-known hierarchy of needs outlines a developmental structure in which human motivations progress from fundamental survival needs (such as food, water, and shelter) to psychological and social needs (including belongingness, esteem, and love), ultimately leading to self-actualization. However, Maslow later revised his model, arguing that self-actualization was not the final stage. Instead, he identified a higher state of being—one that involved transcendent motivations, an innate drive toward experiences that connect individuals with a greater reality beyond the self.

This recognition of growth motivation as a distinct force marked a crucial shift in psychological theory. Unlike deficiency needs, which arise from a sense of lack and are externally driven, growth motivation propels individuals toward experiences of meaning, creativity, and expanded consciousness. Sutich (1966) acknowledged that while humanistic psychology had made significant strides, it failed to capture the depth of inner exploration that cultural traditions had long pursued. He noted that humanistic psychology neglected humanity's place within the broader universe, prompting him to question whether self-actualization alone was an adequate framework for understanding human potential.

Building on Maslow's hierarchy, transpersonal psychologists proposed an expanded model of human development, often conceptualized as four levels of being: (a) the physiological level, (b) the emotional level, (c) the rational level, and (d) the spiritual level. These levels, arranged in ascending order, reflect an increasing degree of psychological complexity and integration. The physiological level, representing survival and bodily needs, forms the foundation. Above it lies the emotional level, encompassing human desires, relationships, and psychological attachments. The rational level, associated with logic, critical thinking, and self-awareness, serves as a bridge to the highest level—the spiritual or transpersonal domain. Here, the self is no longer defined by personal limitations but is understood in relation to a larger, interconnected whole.

Maslow (1976) believed that spiritual values should not be relegated to the realm of supernatural beliefs but should instead be recognized as natural aspects of human development. He argued that spiritual experiences, rather than being anomalies, were intrinsic to the human condition and could be studied scientificall . "We must recognize that spiritual values belong to the domain of human nature and need not be artificially separated from scientific inquiry," he asserted (p. 263). His vision positioned transpersonal psychology within a broader intellectual and existential framework, where the pursuit of meaning, inner growth, and self-transcendence were not peripheral concerns but central elements of psychological inquiry.

Frank (1975) further explored the organic structure of human development, proposing that human experience consists of three interrelated dimensions: body, mind, and spirit. He aligned these dimensions with the four psychological levels described earlier, emphasizing that true psychological integration requires the acknowledgment of all three. The body corresponds to physiological needs, the mind to emotional and rational processes, and the spirit to the self-transcendent dimension. Frank was careful to distinguish his use of spirit from religious connotations, clarifying that it refers to a specific domain of human experience rather than a theological construct. He stressed that without the inclusion of the spiritual dimension, any psychological model would remain incomplete. Maslow (1996) echoed this sentiment, asserting that humans possess a higher level of motivation—one that transcends basic biological and psychological needs and serves as an integral part of their existence.

Guo (2000) synthesized key insights from transpersonal psychology into five fundamental propositions that offer a foundation for further research in this field. These propositions suggest that:

1.The essence of human nature is spiritual. Humans are not merely psychological beings but also possess an innate spiritual dimension that must be acknowledged.

2.Consciousness exists in multiple dimensions. Transpersonal psychology emphasizes the study of expanded states of awareness that go beyond ordinary cognition.

3.Inner life is the source of wisdom. The self is not merely a personal identity but a gateway to deeper, transpersonal knowledge that transcends the ego.

4.Life is inherently meaningful. Transpersonal psychology proposes that the search for meaning is fundamental to psychological well-being and serves as a central component of therapeutic practice.

5.There are multiple paths to spiritual development. A singular, rigid approach to spiritual practice is limiting; instead, transpersonal psychology encourages diverse methods of exploration.

These principles challenge traditional psychological paradigms by suggesting that human identity is not confined to a singular, static self but is instead an evolving, multidimensional process. Rather than viewing consciousness as an isolated phenomenon, transpersonal psychology situates it within a broader, interconnected framework—one that encompasses not only individual experience but also collective and cosmic dimensions of existence.

In bridging psychology, philosophy, and spirituality, transpersonal psychology offers a more expansive view of human potential. It invites us to consider the possibility that our sense of self is not a fixed entity but an unfolding awareness, capable of transcending personal limitations and engaging with the deeper realities of existence. In this sense, transpersonal psychology is not merely an academic discipline but a transformative perspective—one that seeks to integrate scientific rigor with the profound insights of human experience. It challenges us to look beyond conventional psychological models and explore the vast landscapes of consciousness, where the boundaries between self and universe, psychology and spirituality, begin to dissolve.

The Philosophy of Aikido and Mindfulness in Creative Expression

The philosophy of Aikido and mindfulness in creative expression offers a profound intersection between physical movement, psychological resilience, and artistic engagement. While martial arts have long been associated with discipline and self-defense, their deeper impact on mental and emotional states is often overlooked. Aikido, in particular, stands apart from other martial arts due to its philosophical foundation, which emphasizes harmony, adaptability, and the redirection of energy rather than brute force. This principle extends beyond combat; it has the potential to be applied in diverse fields, including performance arts, where actors must cultivate presence, emotional fluidit , and creative spontaneity.

Aikido's emphasis on non-resistance and the fluid integration of movement aligns closely with the psychological states required for effective performance. Unlike other martial arts that prioritize competition and victory, Aikido is rooted in the idea of blending with an opponent's energy, redirecting rather than confronting force. This practice fosters an acute sense of awareness, balance, and adaptability—qualities that are equally valuable to actors navigating the complexities of stage or screen performance. Despite the philosophical and psychological parallels between Aikido and the performing arts, there has been a lack of empirical research exploring their connection. While the psychological benefits of martial arts training have been widely acknowledged, particularly in terms of stress reduction, emotional regulation, and cognitive enhancement, few studies have examined how Aikido's principles could be directly applied to actor training.

This research seeks to address that gap by investigating whether Aikido strategies can generate a form of "spiritual power" that enhances an actor's presence and performance. Through a series of narrative experiments, this study aims to provide empirical evidence regarding the potential relationship between Aikido training and an actor's artistic expression. By comparing the performances of actors who have undergone Aikido training with those who have not, this research explores whether Aikido can serve as an effective preparatory method for actors, not only improving their physical agility and control but also fostering a deeper psychological and emotional engagement with their roles.

Mindfulness meditation, another practice rooted in heightened awareness and self-regulation, complements Aikido in its potential benefits for performance. While Aikido cultivates mindfulness through movement, mindfulness meditation trains the mind in stillness, fostering presence and cognitive flexibilit . The effects of mindfulness meditation are well-documented across both psychological and physiological domains, demonstrating its influence on perception, self-control, value clarification, and emotional regulation. These qualities are essential for actors, who must manage their own psychological states while embodying a wide range of emotions and characters.

From a physiological perspective, mindfulness meditation has been extensively researched in psychology, behavioral science, neuroscience, and health sciences. Interdisciplinary studies have explored its clinical effects, revealing significant benefits in the treatment of chronic pain, anxiety disorders, dermatological conditions, depression relapse, insomnia, substance abuse, alcohol dependence, and cardiovascular diseases. These findings underscore the broader implications of mindfulness beyond stress reduction, positioning it as a transformative tool for enhancing well-being and cognitive performance.

Actors, much like martial artists, rely on their ability to be fully present in the moment, attuned to both internal sensations and external stimuli. The integration of Aikido and mindfulness meditation into performance training represents a holistic approach that merges physical discipline with psychological insight. Just as Aikido practitioners learn to flow with energy rather than resist it, actors can develop a similar responsiveness in their craft—allowing performances to emerge organically rather than being forced. Likewise, mindfulness meditation enables actors to cultivate a deep awareness of their thoughts and emotions, fostering a greater capacity for authenticity and spontaneity on stage.

This study not only highlights the theoretical connections between Aikido, mindfulness, and performance but also seeks to provide practical evidence through experimental research. If the findings support the hypothesis that Aikido training enhances an actor's psychological resilience and creative expression, it could pave the way for a new methodology in actor training—one that incorporates movement-based awareness practices as fundamental components of performance education.

By bridging these disciplines, this research aims to illuminate how ancient wisdom traditions can inform modern artistic practice. The interplay between Aikido's philosophy of harmonious movement and mindfulness meditation's cultivation of inner stillness offers a compelling framework for actors striving to reach deeper levels of presence, authenticity, and emotional fluidity in their work. Performance, in this sense, becomes more than a technical skill—it transforms into a dynamic, embodied process of self-discovery and creative transcendence.

Techniques for Bridging Transpersonal Psychology and Acting

Meditation has long stood at the heart of transpersonal psychology, offering a structured, intentional approach to transcending conventional modes of consciousness. Historically, two primary methods have been recognized for facilitating transpersonal experiences: the use of hallucinogenic agents and the practice of meditation. Both have played crucial roles in expanding the boundaries of psychological inquiry, providing access to altered states of awareness. However, while hallucinogenic substances have demonstrated their capacity to induce profound shifts in perception, their limitations—ranging from unpredictable psychological effects to ethical and physiological concerns—

have rendered them an unreliable and often controversial avenue for research and practice. Meditation, by contrast, has emerged as a more stable and sustainable pathway, offering both a means of self-transcendence and a framework for systematic study.

Meditation's foundational role in transpersonal psychology is widely acknowledged. Walsh and Vaughan (1993) argued that meditation serves as a direct and repeatable method for cultivating expanded states of consciousness, making it indispensable to the field. Unlike chemically induced experiences, which often lack consistency and are subject to external variables, meditation allows individuals to access higher states of awareness through disciplined practice and self-regulation. Its significance extends beyond theoretical discourse; many transpersonal psychologists have themselves engaged in meditative practices, using first-person phenomenological inquiry to deepen their understanding of non-ordinary states of consciousness. This methodological integration of direct experience with empirical study has shaped the very foundations of transpersonal psychology, situating meditation not merely as a subject of investigation but as a primary vehicle for achieving psychological transcendence.

Mindfulness meditation, in particular, has gained prominence due to its systematic approach and its applicability across a range of disciplines, from clinical psychology to cognitive science. It is far more than a passive state of relaxation; rather, it constitutes a dynamic, multi-dimensional process involving perception, self-regulation, value clarificatio , cognitive flexibilit , and emotional resilience. These components are central to the development of transpersonal awareness, enabling individuals to move beyond habitual patterns of thought and behavior toward a more expansive, integrative mode of being.

Perception, in the context of mindfulness, refers to the cultivation of a non-reactive awareness of thoughts, emotions, and external stimuli. Practitioners are trained to observe their experiences without immediate evaluation or attachment, allowing them to recognize cognitive and emotional patterns without being dominated by them. This observational stance is a critical step in the process of self-transcendence, as it enables individuals to engage with their inner world without reinforcing rigid ego structures.

Self-regulation, or the ability to modulate one's internal state in response to external changes, is another cornerstone of mindfulness practice. Unlike conventional forms of self-control, which often rely on suppression or avoidance, mindfulness-based self-regulation emphasizes adaptability and balance. Practitioners develop the capacity to maintain equanimity in the face of shifting mental and emotional states, a skill that is particularly valuable in transpersonal psychology, where the ability to navigate altered states of consciousness without destabilization is essential.

Value clarifica ion plays a similarly crucial role, allowing individuals to discern their most deeply held values and to align their lives accordingly. As meditation practice deepens, practitioners frequently report a reorientation of priorities, in which transient concerns give way to a clearer sense of meaning and purpose. This process reflects one of the fundamental premises of transpersonal psychology: that human consciousness is not solely structured around individualistic or ego-driven needs, but is inherently oriented toward broader, more expansive dimensions of existence.

Cognitive flexibilit , encompassing both emotional and behavioral adaptability, enables practitioners to distinguish between present-moment realities and conditioned responses shaped by past experiences. Through repeated engagement with mindfulness practices, individuals become increasingly capable of responding to situations with clarity and spontaneity rather than being constrained by automatic cognitive and emotional patterns. This flexibility is essential for accessing transpersonal states, as it allows individuals to loosen the rigid self-identifications that often inhibit higher awareness

The final component, exposure, refers to the willingness to confront difficult emotions, memories, and thoughts rather than avoiding or suppressing them. Mindfulness meditation teaches individuals to engage with discomfort in a way that fosters deep psychological integration. By developing the capacity to remain present with challenging experiences, practitioners dismantle the psychological defenses that maintain ego-bound consciousness, thereby opening the door to transpersonal awareness.

These five dimensions—perception, self-regulation, value clarific - tion, cognitive flexibilit , and exposure—constitute the core mechanisms through which mindfulness meditation facilitates psychological transformation. Unlike passive relaxation techniques, mindfulness engages both mind and body in a holistic process aimed at expanding awareness and integrating experience. This alignment with the principles of transpersonal psychology underscores meditation's unique capacity to serve as both a method of inquiry and a tool for personal evolution.

Beyond its individual psychological benefits, meditation also functions as a bridge between psychology, philosophy, and spirituality. Whereas traditional psychological models have often prioritized empirical measurement and behavioral analysis, transpersonal psychology recognizes that certain aspects of consciousness can only be understood through direct experiential engagement. Meditation provides precisely this form of access, allowing for a systematic yet deeply personal exploration of altered states of awareness.

Moreover, meditation's accessibility makes it a particularly valuable transpersonal tool. Unlike pharmacological interventions, which rely on external substances to induce altered states, meditation is an endogenous practice that requires no external manipulation. This renders it both a sustainable and ethically unproblematic method for investigating higher states of consciousness. Additionally, its adaptability across different cultural and spiritual traditions highlights its universality, reinforcing the notion that transpersonal experiences are not confined to any one belief system but are intrinsic to human psychology.

In examining meditation's role within transpersonal psychology, it becomes evident that its significance extends far beyond conventional therapeutic applications. It is not merely a technique for stress reduction or cognitive enhancement; rather, it represents a systematic method for transcending ego-bound consciousness and accessing an expanded, integrative awareness. Whether understood as a psychological discipline, a philosophical inquiry, or a spiritual path, meditation remains one of the most effective and widely studied methods for facilitating transpersonal states.

Ultimately, the study of meditation in transpersonal psychology is not simply an academic pursuit but an invitation to engage with the fundamental nature of consciousness itself. By embracing both empirical analysis and direct experience, transpersonal psychology challenges us to reconsider the boundaries of human potential. Meditation, in this context, is not merely a subject of study but a transformative process—one that continues to shape our understanding of what it means to move beyond the self, toward a deeper, more expansive engagement with reality.

Chapter 3

Paths of Inquiry and Exploration

Framing the Approach: A Philosophical and Methodological Foundation

Why This Path? Justifying the Framework

The connection between transpersonal psychology and dramatic performance is both profound and multifaceted. Performance is more than a craft—it is an immersive experience that demands an alignment of body, mind, and presence. At its highest level, acting is not merely a mechanical execution of learned techniques but an art of embodiment and transcendence, where the performer channels emotions, dissolves personal boundaries, and inhabits a character beyond their ordinary sense of self. The ability to achieve such deep states of engagement is not solely dependent on talent or technique but is fundamentally infl - enced by the actor's psychological state. This book explores how transpersonal psychological practices, particularly aikido and mindfulness meditation, can serve as powerful tools to cultivate this heightened awareness and transform artistic expression.

At the heart of this exploration lies a structured comparative study, designed to reveal the internal relationships between transpersonal psychology and acting. The study examined the impact of transpersonal psychological methods on actor performance by comparing participants who had engaged in aikido and mindfulness meditation with those who had not. The contrast between these two groups was not just intended to measure differences in technical ability but to assess shifts in consciousness, emotional depth, and overall stage presence. The effectiveness of these interventions was not judged solely on subjective interpretation but was evaluated through audience perception and performance assessment, offering both empirical evidence and qualitative insights into the transformative potential of transpersonal practices in acting.

The theoretical foundation of this approach is rooted in established research on transpersonal states and artistic creativity. Mindfulness meditation, widely recognized as a gateway to expanded awareness, has been shown to facilitate states of cognitive clarity, emotional balance, and presence, all of which are critical for an actor's performance. The practice of aikido, originating from Eastern martial traditions, fosters fluid movement, heightened body awareness, and a philosophy of non-resistance, aligning closely with transpersonal psychology's emphasis on the dissolution of ego-boundaries and the experience of flo . Given these shared principles, aikido and mindfulness meditation were not arbitrarily chosen but were deliberately integrated into this study as structured interventions to explore their potential impact on artistic performance.

To ensure the validity of the comparison, participants remained consistent across all experimental stages. Each individual performed twice— once before any exposure to transpersonal psychological methods and once after engaging in aikido and mindfulness training. This methodological consistency ensured that any observed changes in performance, presence, and expressive capability could be attributed to the intervention itself rather than external factors. The uniformity of participants between these phases provided a controlled framework for assessing variations in consciousness and behavior, allowing for a precise examination of how these transpersonal methods influence the artistic process.

The study was designed in three sequential stages, reflecting a progressive integration of transpersonal techniques into performance practice. In the first stage, actors performed without any intervention, offering a baseline assessment of their abilities, habitual patterns, and engagement with the craft. This initial stage was critical in establishing a reference point against which later transformations could be compared. The second stage introduced the intervention—actors were immersed in structured training sessions involving mindfulness meditation and aikido practice. These methods were not merely included as supplementary exercises but were fundamental components of the experiment, intended to reshape the way participants approached their craft. The final stage involved a post-intervention performance, allowing participants to apply the skills and awareness cultivated through transpersonal practices. Audience evaluations, coupled with self-reflections from the participants, provided valuable insights into how these methods altered their experience of performance.

Beyond its immediate application to acting, this study underscores a broader paradigm in the intersection of transpersonal psychology and artistic transformation. Transpersonal psychology, having emerged as an extension of humanistic psychology, has long been recognized for its role in expanding states of consciousness, fostering peak experiences, and facilitating self-transcendence. While much of its research has centered on therapeutic settings, its potential in the creative arts has remained largely unexplored. Yet, performance itself is inherently transpersonal—actors are required to step beyond their individual selves, embody alternate realities, and immerse themselves in heightened emotional and psychological states. This study positions transpersonal psychology not as an external influence on acting but as a natural extension of what performers already experience, providing structured pathways to enter flow states and sustain a deeper, more authentic artistic presence.

The implications of these findings extend far beyond acting. The concept of presence, emotional fluidit , and self-transcendence applies not only to theater but to all forms of creative and expressive engagement. Musicians, dancers, athletes, and even public speakers operate within similar psychological and embodied dynamics, where performance is not simply a matter of skill but an interplay of awareness, responsiveness, and deep immersion. The principles observed in this research suggest that training in transpersonal methods may serve as a valuable tool for any discipline that requires individuals to operate at their peak, in states of fluid, embodied creativit .

More than just a study of technique and methodology, this book is a testament to the profound impact of transpersonal awareness on the performing arts. Acting, when viewed through the lens of transpersonal psychology, is not merely about playing a role—it is about engaging with the depths of human experience, embracing the full spectrum of consciousness, and transforming one's state of being in service of artistic expression. The stage, much like the meditative space, offers a setting where selfhood dissolves, where presence is absolute, and where one can exist, even if momentarily, in a state beyond the constraints of ordinary perception.

By drawing from Eastern contemplative traditions, embodied movement practices, and psychological research, this book brings forth a new perspective on what it means to act, to perform, and to be fully present. It challenges traditional notions of acting as mere technique and instead positions performance as a profoundly psychological and transpersonal process, where artistic mastery is not only about skill, but about deep inner transformation. The findings presented here offer a glimpse into how transpersonal awareness can refine not just artistic ability, but the entire way in which actors—and indeed, all creative individuals—engage with their craft and themselves.

Through the structured integration of aikido and mindfulness meditation, this work does not merely present a theoretical analysis but provides a practical model for cultivating presence, depth, and transcendence in artistic performance. The revelations within these pages serve as both an invitation and a challenge—an invitation to reimagine the psychological dimensions of performance and a challenge to adopt a more holistic approach to artistic development, one that integrates body, mind, and consciousness in the pursuit of artistic and personal transformation.

A Guiding Structure for Discovery

At its core, this study sought to examine how transpersonal psychological practices—specifically aikido and mindfulness meditation—influence an actor's performance quality, stage presence, and artistic expression. To investigate this, a structured experimental design was developed, incorporating dramatic performance assessments, audience evaluations, and transpersonal psychological interventions. Unlike traditional performance studies that focus solely on external aspects such as technique and delivery, this research explored the internal transformation of actors, considering how altered states of consciousness, heightened bodily awareness, and deeper emotional engagement contribute to performance outcomes.

The study was structured in three sequential stages, allowing for a progressive integration of transpersonal techniques into performance practice. In the first stage, participants engaged in an initial performance of a selected dramatic piece. Two carefully chosen dramatic works served as the experimental material, providing a structured yet expressive framework for the actors' engagement. A designated group of professional evaluators, experienced in theatrical analysis, observed the performances and provided quantitative and qualitative assessments of the actors' engagement, presence, and overall effectiveness. This phase established a baseline measure, capturing each participant's performance in its natural, untrained state.

Following this initial assessment, the second stage introduced the transpersonal psychological intervention. Participants were immersed in structured aikido and mindfulness meditation training, guided by experienced instructors specializing in both performance training and transpersonal psychology. These practices were not merely supplemental exercises but integrated methodologies, intended to cultivate deeper embodied awareness, emotional regulation, and creative spontaneity—qualities essential to both acting and self-transcendence. The aikido training emphasized fluid, non-resistant movement, reinforcing the principles of grace, energy flo , and responsive engagement with space and fellow performers. Meanwhile, mindfulness meditation trained participants in sustained present-moment awareness, allowing them to enter a state of deep psychological immersion necessary for authentic dramatic expression.

The third stage required participants to engage in a second round of performances, this time applying the insights and awareness cultivated through their transpersonal training. A new dramatic piece was introduced to prevent mere memorization from influencing performance quality. Once again, professional evaluators assessed the performances, providing a second set of scores to compare against the initial baseline. This structured sequence of performance, training, and re-performance allowed for a clear and methodologically rigorous exploration of how transpersonal practices impact dramatic artistry.

A critical component of this research was the dual-contrast experimental design, which provided two distinct comparative frameworks. The first level of contrast involved a within-subject comparison, analyzing how each participant's performance changed from the first to the second staged drama. Because the same evaluators assessed both performances, it was possible to isolate and measure the impact of the intervention, focusing on changes in emotional depth, stage presence, and psychological absorption.

The second level of contrast involved between-group comparisons, enabling an analysis of how different participants responded to transpersonal interventions based on their previous experience in performance. Participants were selected according to deliberate variation criteria, ensuring that the study included both experienced actors and novice performers. This distinction was crucial, as it allowed for an examination of whether the effects of transpersonal psychological training were equally beneficial across different skill levels or whether experienced actors displayed a different mode of transformation compared to those less trained in performance. By structuring the study in this way, the research was able to explore not only the general efficacy of transpersonal practices but also their nuanced effects across diverse artistic backgrounds.

The design of this study was not purely mechanistic; it was built upon the philosophy that acting is not just about external technique but about a deeper, almost spiritual engagement with the craft. Through this methodological framework, the research does not merely measure changes in acting ability—it seeks to illuminate the profound psychological shifts that occur when actors are trained to embody fluidit , mindfulness, and transpersonal awareness. By using aikido and mindfulness meditation as a means of training not just the body, but also the mind and spirit, this work contributes to a broader understanding of how artistic practice can be transformed through conscious, embodied awareness.

What emerges from this investigation is a compelling intersection of psychology, philosophy, and performance theory. This research does not simply present an experiment—it tells a narrative of transformation, a structured journey that mirrors the very arc of dramatic storytelling itself. Actors, much like the characters they portray, undergo a process of awakening, challenge, and resolution. The transpersonal training functions as a catalyst for artistic and personal evolution, offering insights not only for performers but for anyone seeking to engage more fully with the present moment, the body, and the depth of human expression.

Validity, Reliability, and the Challenges of Interpretation

Ensuring the validity of this research required careful consideration of multiple factors that could potentially influence the experimental outcomes. Two primary challenges emerged in this regard: the experimental environment and the energy levels of participants and audience members. Both elements had the potential to introduce inconsistencies or unintended variables into the study, necessitating thoughtful design measures to minimize bias and enhance the reliability of findings

The experimental environment played a crucial role in shaping the conditions under which the transpersonal psychological interventions—aikido and mindfulness meditation—were conducted. These practices require a heightened state of focused awareness, making environmental control a key consideration. To ensure that participants could engage deeply with the practice, training sessions were conducted in a controlled and enclosed space, shielded from external distractions. This approach provided an optimal setting for introspection, embodied awareness, and psychological immersion, all of which are fundamental to the effectiveness of transpersonal methods. Since both aikido and mindfulness meditation require sustained attention and deep concentration, an environment free from unnecessary external stimuli was essential in facilitating authentic engagement with the practice.

To further enhance methodological integrity, professional instructors specializing in aikido and mindfulness meditation were brought in to guide participants through the training process. This measure served a dual purpose. First, it ensured that the techniques were implemented correctly, reducing variability in how participants engaged with the transpersonal methods. Second, the presence of experienced facilitators helped to standardize the intervention, ensuring that all participants received consistent instruction, thereby minimizing discrepancies in individual practice quality. By curating both the physical and instructional environment, the research design effectively safeguarded against uncontrolled variables that might otherwise compromise the validity of the findings

Beyond environmental factors, another critical consideration was the energy levels of participants and audience members—an often-overlooked yet fundamental aspect in performance-based research. The contrast experiment model, by its very nature, required participants to engage in physically and emotionally demanding performances twice, first before any transpersonal intervention and then after aikido and mindfulness training. This repetition posed a risk: participant fatigue could potentially influence performance quality, independent of the effects of the intervention itself. Recognizing this, the study was strategically designed to incorporate a rest period between the initial performance and the transpersonal practice phase. This interval allowed participants to recover both physically and mentally, ensuring that any observed changes in performance could be attributed to the psychological and physiological effects of aikido and mindfulness rather than mere exhaustion.

Similarly, the audience's ability to assess performances consistently was another factor that required careful regulation. Watching multiple performances within a short timeframe could lead to cognitive fatigue or desensitization, potentially affecting the accuracy of evaluations. To mitigate this, the study ensured that audience members were given adequate breaks and recalibration periods between assessments, allowing them to maintain attentional engagement and critical judgment throughout the evaluation process.

By addressing these potential threats to validity, the research design upheld rigorous methodological standards, ensuring that findings were not skewed by environmental inconsistencies, fatigue-related bias, or variability in participant engagement. Rather than viewing these challenges as mere obstacles, they were integrated into the research design as essential variables requiring strategic management. This approach underscores the complex, multidimensional nature of performance-based research, where both internal (psychological and physiological) and external (environmental and procedural) factors must be carefully orchestrated to yield meaningful and reliable insights into the transformative power of transpersonal psychology in artistic expression.

Tools for Understanding: Methods of Inquiry

Mapping the Landscape of Existing Measurement Tools:

The research presented in this book employed a combination of contrast experiments, questionnaire-based data collection, and statistical analysis as its primary methodological tools, each playing a critical role in verifying the proposed findings. The study was structured to ensure a rigorous, multidimensional approach, integrating empirical observation, subjective participant feedback, and quantitative statistical validation to provide a comprehensive understanding of the effects of transpersonal psychological interventions on artistic performance.

Contrast experiments formed the foundation of this study, allowing for a direct comparison of performance variations before and after exposure to aikido and mindfulness meditation. This experimental design was critical in identifying measurable differences in actors' stage presence, emotional depth, and cognitive engagement following transpersonal training. By using a within-subject comparison, where the same individuals performed both before and after the intervention, and a between-group analysis, which examined variations among participants with different levels of prior acting experience, the study ensured that the results were not only reflective of individual transformations but also indicative of broader trends in artistic development.

In addition to the experimental assessments, questionnaire-based data collection provided a subjective yet indispensable dimension to the research. Performance, particularly in artistic disciplines, cannot be fully evaluated through external observation alone; the inner experience of the performer plays a crucial role in shaping their artistic expression. The questionnaires were designed to capture self-reported experiences, perceptual shifts, and cognitive-emotional changes in participants, allowing for an analysis of the psychological impact of aikido and mindfulness meditation on the creative process. By integrating qualitative reflections with quantitative performance assessments, this research sought to correlate internal cognitive and emotional shifts with observable artistic expression, offering insights into the mind-body interplay in performance training and statistical analysis was employed to validate the empirical findings, ensuring that observed patterns were not merely coincidental or anecdotal but were statistically significant and theoretically robust. Performance evaluation, often viewed as inherently subjective, was made more empirically grounded through the use of structured audience assessments, rating scales, and comparative statistical methods. This analytical approach reinforced the credibility of the study, ensuring that the relationship between transpersonal psychology and artistic performance could be examined through a combination of experiential, behavioral, and numerical data.

Beyond its immediate methodological structure, this research was guided by a holistic epistemological perspective, acknowledging that performance is not simply a set of technical skills but a complex, embodied, and psychologically intricate process. The integration of contrast experiments, self-report data, and statistical verification allowed for a nuanced investigation into how transpersonal training reshapes an actor's creative awareness, emotional fluidit , and embodied presence.

This book's research was designed to verify the proposed results through methods as follows:

Experimentation, Observation, and the Role of Context

Among the vast array of research methodologies, contrast experiments stand out as one of the most illuminating approaches, offering a structured way to explore causality, correlation, and the nuanced interplay of influential factors. By systematically controlling variables, contrast experiments allow researchers to dissect the impact of specific influences, thereby revealing patterns that might otherwise remain obscured. Their power lies not only in their ability to provide empirical clarity but also in their capacity to provoke deeper theoretical refle - tions on the nature of psychological and behavioral phenomena.

In the context of this study, contrast experiments were employed extensively, serving as a cornerstone for analysis. These experiments unfolded across two primary dimensions, each designed to illuminate different facets of the research question. The first dimension encompassed a broader comparative framework, distinguishing between participants who had been exposed to transpersonal psychological methods and those who had not. This contrast provided a foundation for assessing the tangible effects of such interventions, offering insights into the degree and nature of their influence. By systematically gathering data from both groups, the research was able to delineate how transpersonal psychological methods shaped individuals' cognitive, emotional, and behavioral responses, thereby contributing to a more comprehensive understanding of their efficac .

The second dimension of the contrast experiments delved deeper, focusing on internal variations among participants. Here, the goal was to explore how transpersonal psychological interventions interacted with diverse individual conditions, including professional background, gender, geographic origin, and age. These internal contrasts were particularly revealing, as they shed light on the differential impact of the same psychological methods across various demographic and contextual factors. For instance, did individuals from different cultural backgrounds respond similarly to transpersonal interventions? Were certain age groups more receptive than others? How did professional experience shape the learning outcomes associated with these methods? Such questions were at the heart of this experimental approach, enabling a more refined and multidimensional understanding of psychological influence

What makes contrast experiments particularly compelling is their ability to move beyond mere statistical comparisons. They offer a dynamic way of thinking about influence and change, one that acknowledges the complexity of human psychology while striving for empirical rigor. In this study, contrast experiments did not merely serve as a technical tool; they became a lens through which the intricate dance between intervention and individual difference could be observed with greater clarity. Through carefully structured comparisons, they provided a rich, layered narrative—one that not only quantifie effects but also invited reflection on the deeper mechanisms at pla .

Ultimately, contrast experiments are more than just a method; they are a way of seeing. By juxtaposing different conditions, they reveal the often-subtle ways in which change occurs, offering insights that transcend the confines of data points and statistics. In the case of transpersonal psychological methods, their use in this study provided a compelling exploration of influence—one that speaks to both the precision of scientific inquiry and the broader quest for understanding human transformation.

Designing Surveys and Capturing Subjective Experience

To assess the psychological impact of transpersonal psychological methods—including aikido and mindfulness meditation—on participants, closed-ended questions were selected and incorporated into the study. The primary objective of this questionnaire-based assessment was to capture variations in participants' psychological states following the intervention. By systematically evaluating responses, the study aimed to identify the extent to which transpersonal practices infl - enced individual participants and to establish a data-driven framework for comparison.

The questionnaire was carefully structured with an internal logical sequence, ensuring that responses provided a coherent and interpretable measure of psychological transformation. Participants who selected positive responses were understood to have experienced a higher degree of influence from the transpersonal psychological intervention, indicating a greater degree of engagement with the methods and their transformative effects. Conversely, those whose responses indicated minimal or no perceptible change were categorized as having not been significantly affected by the intervention. This categorization allowed for a clear division of participants into two primary groups: those who demonstrated a strong psychological response to the training and those for whom the intervention did not result in noticeable psychological shifts.

The final stage of this process involved the formation of contrast groups based on questionnaire data. These groups were essential for further analysis, allowing the study to compare and contrast the effects of transpersonal practices across different participants. By integrating quantitative assessment through structured responses with qualitative interpretation, the research ensured that subjective psychological experiences were systematically categorized and analyzed. This methodological approach not only strengthened the validity of the experimental design but also offered deeper insights into the mechanisms through which transpersonal psychological methods influence artistic performance and psychological states.

Statistical and Thematic Analysis: Making Sense of the Data

This book's research employed a range of statistical analysis methods to examine the data collected from both participants and audience evaluations. Given the multifaceted nature of the study, different statistical techniques were applied at various stages, ensuring that the data were analyzed with precision and methodological rigor.

For performance assessments, comparative statistical methods were used to evaluate the differences between pre- and post-intervention performances. By analyzing audience evaluation scores, this research aimed to determine whether actors exhibited significant improvements in stage presence, emotional depth, and expressive engagement after undergoing transpersonal psychological training. The application of descriptive and inferential statistical techniques allowed for an objective measurement of performance variations, helping to distinguish genuine effects of the intervention from random fluctuations in performance quality.

For questionnaire data, statistical methods were utilized to classify and interpret patterns of psychological change among participants. Techniques such as frequency distribution analysis, correlation analysis, and group comparisons were applied to explore the extent to which individuals were influenced by aikido and mindfulness meditation. By structuring the responses into distinct categories—those who exhibited strong psychological shifts versus those who did not—the study was able to form statistically valid contrast groups for further comparison.

Recognizing that different aspects of this book's research required distinct analytical approaches, the study integrated both parametric and non-parametric statistical tests, depending on the nature of the data. This approach ensured that qualitative insights derived from audience perception and self-reported experiences were quantitatively validated, reinforcing the scientific credibility and empirical robustness of the findings. Through this structured statistical framework, this research provided a comprehensive, data-driven analysis of the transformative impact of transpersonal psychological methods on acting performance.

Learning from Prior Research and Comparative Studies

In the field of scientific research, contrast experiments have become a widely adopted method, particularly in studies requiring the comparison of at least two groups. This approach is designed to explore differences between experimental and control groups by manipulating an independent variable, ensuring that the observed outcomes are directly linked to the intervention being studied. In the realm of transpersonal psychology, contrast experiments have been frequently employed to investigate the psychological and physiological effects of mindfulness meditation on individuals. Many previous studies have utilized this methodology, particularly in examining mindfulness-based interventions such as Mindfulness-Based Stress Reduction (MBSR), Mindfulness-Based Cognitive Therapy (MBCT), and Dialectical Behavior Therapy (DBT).

Empirical research has demonstrated the efficacy of mindfulness-based interventions through contrast experimental designs. Wong (2015) conducted a study on 216 patients suffering from insomnia, concluding that MBCT was more effective in alleviating insomnia than traditional psychoeducation. The study divided participants into experimental and control groups to examine the impact of mindfulness meditation on various psychological conditions, including emotional regulation,

anxiety, and chronic pain management. Similarly, Baer (2003) recruit-
ed 28 participants, dividing them equally into experimental and control
groups. Findings revealed that those in the experimental group, who
received MBSR-based intervention, exhibited enhanced emotional
regulation, reduced psychological stress, and a significant decrease in
negative emotions. Bamhofer (2007) conducted another notable study,
selecting 31 patients diagnosed with depressive disorder as the experimental sample. Through contrast experiments, the study confirmed
that MBCT significantly alleviated depressive symptoms, providing
empirical evidence supporting the therapeutic effects of mindfulness
meditation. These studies highlight the effectiveness of contrast experiments in validating the psychological and physiological benefits
of transpersonal interventions.

In addition to contrast experiments, questionnaires have been widely
used as a research instrument for data collection, particularly in social sciences. The primary advantage of questionnaire-based research
lies in its efficienc , objectivity, and ability to capture the perspectives of a specific population within a short timeframe. Across various disciplines, researchers have employed questionnaires to gath-
er quantitative and qualitative insights, making it an essential tool in
psychological and social research. In previous studies on transpersonal psychology, questionnaires have been utilized to investigate
the transformative effects of transpersonal psychological interventions on individuals. However, existing research has not extensively
explored the use of questionnaires to assess participants' experiences
after engaging in transpersonal methods such as aikido and mindfulness meditation. This book's research addresses this gap by integrating
questionnaire-based assessment as a means of capturing participants'

psychological and experiential transformations following transpersonal training.

Furthermore, statistical analysis has been a foundational tool in processing large-scale data across various research fields, including psychology, education, and behavioral sciences. Despite its broad applicability, few previous studies in transpersonal psychology have applied statistical methods to analyze actors' performance outcomes. In this book's research, data collection relied primarily on audience evaluation scores and questionnaire responses from participants. Through rigorous statistical analysis, this study aims to strengthen the empirical validity of its findings, offering scientifically robust evidence on the impact of transpersonal psychological training on artistic performance. By incorporating contrast experiments, structured questionnaires, and statistical evaluation, this research seeks to contribute a more data-driven and systematic understanding of how transpersonal interventions influence an acto 's craft.

The Process of Engagement

Phases of Inquiry: From Initial Exploration to Deeper Investigation.

To ensure that the experimental design was both effective and valid, the study was conducted in two distinct stages, allowing for a progressive refinement of methodology and implementation. This structured approach ensured that potential methodological limitations were identified and addressed before conducting the full-scale research

The first stage was the pilot study, designed to test the feasibility and validity of the experimental framework using a limited sample size.

This phase served as a preliminary assessment, allowing for adjustments to the experimental structure, data collection procedures, and intervention protocols. The pilot study played a critical role in refining the research methodology, ensuring that the experimental conditions were optimized for reliable and replicable results in the subsequent formal study.

The second stage was the formal study, in which the finalized experimental design was fully implemented. This phase was structured into multiple steps, each carefully designed to systematically measure the effects of transpersonal psychological interventions on participants' performance. Through this multi-stage experimental approach, the research aimed to generate robust, scientifically sound conclusions, ensuring that the findings were both theoretically rigorous and empirically validated.

The preliminary study was conducted at Sofia University in February 2018 with five participants, all of whom had prior experience in dramatic performance. The primary objective of this phase was to examine the impact of transpersonal psychological interventions, specifically aikido and mindfulness meditation, and to determine whether the experimental design was methodologically sound. The study was intentionally structured in a simplified format to evaluate the fundamental assumptions before expanding to a larger sample.

Step 1: The five participants performed a short dramatic piece lasting approximately three minutes. Their performances were evaluated by three experienced audience members, all of whom were senior learners in performance studies. Each evaluator provided a quantitative performance score based on predefined assessment criteria

Step 2: Following the initial performance, the five participants engaged in aikido and mindfulness meditation training, guided by a qualified instructor specializing in transpersonal psychological methods. This intervention phase lasted for ten minutes, during which participants practiced embodied movement techniques, mindfulness exercises, and awareness-based training to enhance presence, emotional regulation, and expressive fluidit .

Step 3: After the intervention, participants performed another brief dramatic piece, again lasting approximately three minutes. The same three audience members provided a second set of performance evaluations, using the same scoring criteria to maintain assessment consistency.

The data collected from the audience evaluation scores indicated that the second performance scores were significantly higher than those from the first. Four out of the five participants demonstrated notable improvements, with performance scores reflecting greater emotional depth, enhanced stage presence, and increased fluidity in expression. Statistical analysis at this stage focused on comparing performance outcomes before and after the intervention, measuring the immediate effects of aikido and mindfulness meditation on artistic expression.

The findings from this preliminary study provided strong initial evidence that transpersonal psychological methods—including aikido and mindfulness meditation—had a measurable impact on acting performance. More importantly, these results validated the fundamental design of the research, confirming its effectiveness and methodological robustness and providing a solid foundation for the formal study.

Selecting and Understanding Participants

The participants in this study were drawn from a pool of volunteers with at least one year of acting and performance training experience. While the initial selection was conducted randomly, it followed specific eligibility criteria to ensure the integrity of the experiment. One key requirement was that all participants must never have practiced aikido or mindfulness meditation before. This was not a trivial detail—it was essential to the research design. Prior exposure to these transpersonal psychological methods could introduce uncontrolled variables, making it difficult to measure their true impact. If participants had already engaged in aikido or mindfulness training, they might bring pre-existing familiarity with mind-body awareness techniques, potentially influencing their performance independent of the intervention. To avoid this, the selection process strictly ensured that no participant had any background in these practices.

A total of 40 valid participants were needed, striking a balance between statistical reliability and practical feasibility. This number was chosen carefully—not too small to risk weak data, but not so large as to make the study unwieldy. The goal was to create a consistent baseline while allowing for a rich exploration of individual differences in acting experience, demographics, and cultural backgrounds.

Group Assignment: Designing Meaningful Contrasts

To fully explore the potential impact of transpersonal psychological interventions, the 40 selected participants were divided into four contrast groups. Each group was designed to examine a specific variable, allowing for a more nuanced understanding of how aikido and mindfulness meditation might influence actors' performance. Each group contained 10 participants, a manageable number that ensured enough variation for meaningful comparison while maintaining internal consistency.

Group 1: Experience-Based Contrast

Acting, like any craft, develops over time. But does experience level affect how actors respond to transpersonal training?

Five participants were selected from those with more than three years of acting training—they were the senior learners.

The other five had less than one year of acting experience—they were the junior learners.

The goal was to determine whether seasoned actors absorbed transpersonal techniques differently than those new to the craft. Would experienced actors integrate aikido and mindfulness into their performances more seamlessly, or would newer actors, with fewer ingrained habits, be more receptive?

Group 2: Gender-Based Contrast

Gender is often overlooked in performance research, yet it can shape how people engage with embodiment, presence, and emotional regulation.

Five participants were male, and five were female

This group was designed to explore whether gender differences played a role in how actors internalized transpersonal training. Would men and women experience the same depth of transformation? Would they engage differently with aikido's fluid movements or mindfulness's introspective focus?

Group 3: Cultural Background Contrast

Culture deeply influences how people relate to their bodies, emotions, and personal expression.

Five participants were from Western countries, such as the United States. The other five were from Eastern countries, such as China

The purpose was to examine whether cultural background influenced the way actors responded to transpersonal psychological methods.

Given that Eastern traditions have long embraced meditation and embodied movement, while Western traditions often emphasize psychological realism and external technique, this contrast aimed to reveal whether actors' receptivity to aikido and mindfulness differed across cultural conditioning.

Group 4: Age-Based Contrast

Age brings different strengths to the actor's craft—youth often lends physical flexibility and adaptability, while maturity brings deeper emotional intelligence.

Five participants were aged 35–50, and the other five were 20–35

This group was designed to see whether age influenced the effectiveness of transpersonal training. Would older actors be more resistant to new practices, or would their emotional depth allow for greater transformation? Would younger actors, often more physically agile, find aikido's movement-based approach more intuitive?

Each of these groupings was more than just a way to categorize participants; they were intentional contrasts designed to uncover how different personal factors shape the effectiveness of transpersonal interventions in acting.

Selecting the right participants for the study was only half of the equation. Just as important was choosing the right audience members to evaluate the performances. If the evaluation process lacked consistency, the study would be compromised.

To ensure fair and professional assessments, 10 audience members were carefully selected. All evaluators were performance majors from the same university, ensuring that their critiques were informed by a shared understanding of acting principles. This wasn't a casual audience; these were individuals trained to observe acting with a critical and professional eye.

The decision to select evaluators from the same academic environment was deliberate. Since they were all trained in similar methodologies, they were likely to share common evaluative standards, reducing the risk of subjective bias. Without this consistency, evaluations could become unreliable, with each judge applying entirely different criteria to their assessments.

Additionally, the use of trained evaluators helped eliminate the potential influence of untrained observer bias. A general audience might rely on personal taste rather than objective performance metrics. By choosing senior learners in performance studies, the research ensured that assessments focused on technical precision, emotional depth, and authenticity rather than personal preference.

The participant selection and group assignment process was not just about who participated but about how the study could uncover deeper insights. By accounting for factors like acting experience, gender, cultural background, and age, the research was able to explore not only whether transpersonal training impacts acting performance but also how different individuals experience and integrate these practices.

This approach wasn't just about ensuring methodological rigor; it was about making meaningful discoveries. Would a Western actor struggle with mindfulness in a way that an Eastern actor might not? Would a senior learner resist aikido's fluidit , while a beginner embraced it with ease? These were the kinds of real-world questions that this study sought to answer.

By structuring the participant pool in a way that allowed for deeper exploration, this research aimed to generate insights that extend beyond a single experiment, offering a more profound understanding of how transpersonal psychology and performance training intersect.

Structuring the Investigation: Steps and Considerations

To systematically explore the effects of transpersonal psychological interventions, the experimental process was divided into four major steps, with each step corresponding to one of the contrast groups. This structured approach allowed for precise comparisons between participants with different backgrounds and ensured that the study could effectively analyze how variables such as experience level, gender, cultural background, and age influenced the impact of transpersonal training.

Step 1: Initial Performance Assessment

Each participant was assigned a unique identification number from 01 to 40, categorizing them into the four predefined contrast groups as follows:

1.Performance Experience Group:

Participants No.1–5: Senior learners (actors with more than three years of training)

Participants No.6–10: Junior learners (actors with less than one year of training)

2.Gender Group:

Participants No.11–15: Female actors

Participants No.16–20: Male actors

3.Cultural Background Group:

Participants No.21–25: Actors from Eastern countries

Participants No.26–30: Actors from Western countries

4.Age Group:

Participants No.31–35: Actors aged 35–50

Participants No.36–40: Actors aged 20–35

Each participant was required to perform a monologue from Scene 1 of Act III in Hamlet (see Appendix A). This iconic soliloquy, "To be or not to be," was chosen due to its universal recognition and rich emotional depth, allowing for a meaningful assessment of acting ability, emotional expression, and stage presence. Participants were given three hours to prepare before their performance.

The selection of the experimental drama script was based on familiarity and accessibility. Since Hamlet is widely studied in acting programs, it provided a common reference point that ensured participants
could focus on performance quality rather than script comprehension.
To accommodate different linguistic preferences, both the modern English adaptation and the original Shakespearean text were provided.
Participants had the flexibilit to choose whichever version best suited
their interpretative style, allowing for greater authenticity in their performances.

At this stage, no participant had yet received any transpersonal psychological interventions, such as aikido or mindfulness meditation.
They performed without any external guidance from acting coaches
or transpersonal psychology instructors, allowing their natural acting
tendencies to emerge. This baseline assessment served as a preliminary measure of their performance ability before the intervention.

Following each performance, the ten audience evaluators provided individual performance ratings using a 10-point scale, where:

1 represented the lowest level of audience satisfaction,

10 represented the highest level of audience satisfaction.

The audience evaluators assessed performances independently, ensuring that subjective bias was minimized and that each performance was
evaluated based on standardized criteria. A sample evaluation score
table (see Table 1) was used to record these scores systematically.

This step established a baseline for comparison, allowing the study to later assess the impact of transpersonal psychological interventions by comparing pre- and post-intervention performances. By ensuring that all participants performed under the same conditions and without prior exposure to transpersonal techniques, the research maintained methodological rigor and validity, setting the stage for the next phase of the investigation. The evaluation score table sample was the Table 1 as follows:

Table 1   Evaluation Score Table before Transpersonal Psychological Practice

Participants No.	Group No.	Score(1-10)
01	1	XX
02	1	XX
...	...	...

To ensure the integrity of the experimental results, audience members were strictly prohibited from interacting with participants throughout the entire process. This measure was implemented to eliminate potential biases and maintain the validity of the evaluation. Performance scores were collected immediately after each session, ensuring that the assessments reflected the unfiltered impressions of the evaluator

Following the first performance assessment (Step 1), participants were given a full day of rest to allow for physical and mental recuperation before engaging in the next phase of the study. This intentional break was not merely logistical but was designed to ensure that any performance improvements observed later could be attributed to transpersonal psychological training rather than fatigue, cognitive overload, or external factors.

Step 2: Transpersonal Psychological Training – Aikido and Mindfulness Meditation

In this phase, all participants underwent structured training in transpersonal psychological methods, specifically aikido and mindfulness meditation. These practices were not introduced casually; they were guided by professional instructors specializing in each discipline, ensuring that participants received authentic, structured, and methodologically sound training. This step was carefully designed to allow participants to fully engage with the techniques before applying them in their second performance assessment.

This stage was divided into four sub-steps, each progressively leading participants into a deeper state of transpersonal awareness and embodied practice.

Sub-Step 1: Initial Engagement with Mindfulness Meditation

All 40 participants gathered in a designated quiet space at Sofia University, where they were introduced to the fundamentals of mindfulness meditation. A certified mindfulness meditation instructor led this session, ensuring a methodical and immersive entry into the practice. The focus of this stage was not to achieve profound meditative states immediately but rather to gently guide participants into a receptive and present-centered mindset.

The instructor used verbal cues, breath awareness techniques, and guided relaxation to facilitate a smooth transition into meditative awareness, helping participants move beyond surface-level concentration into a deeper sense of inner stillness and focus.

Sub-Step 2: Deepening the Mindfulness Meditation Practice

Once participants were familiarized with the foundational aspects of mindfulness, they were guided into a more profound meditative state—a critical phase of the mindfulness meditation intervention. This process lasted 30 minutes and was carefully structured as follows:

1.Participants assumed a traditional seated meditation posture, sitting cross-legged with eyes gently closed.

2.Each participant selected a focal point for attention—they could choose between the breath, a specific word (mantra), or an external sound.

3.A structured breathing exercise was introduced, where participants practiced deep diaphragmatic breathing for one minute to cultivate a relaxed and centered state.

4.Guided focus training followed, instructing participants to anchor their awareness to their chosen focal point and maintain this focus throughout the session.

5.Distraction management techniques were taught, emphasizing that if the mind wandered, participants were to gently and non-judgmentally return their attention to their chosen focal point, reinforcing the principles of non-attachment and mental discipline.

By structuring the meditation process in this progressive manner, the study ensured that all participants, regardless of prior meditative experience, could meaningfully engage with the practice. This phase cultivated heightened presence, emotional balance, and cognitive clarity, forming a psychological foundation for the subsequent aikido training.

Sub-Step 3: Transition to a Relaxed and Open State

The conclusion of the mindfulness meditation session was designed to help participants gradually emerge from deep meditation while maintaining a state of inner calm and heightened awareness. The instructor carefully guided the transition, ensuring that participants did not experience mental disorientation or abrupt shifts in consciousness.

Following this step, participants were given a 10-minute break, allowing time to integrate their meditative state before transitioning into the aikido practice. This interval served an essential purpose: rather than treating meditation and aikido as separate, compartmentalized practices, the break allowed participants to carry their meditative awareness into the next stage of training, fostering continuity between mental stillness and physical movement.

Sub-Step 4: Introduction to Aikido Training

With the mental foundation established through meditation, participants now engaged in aikido training, shifting from internal psychological work to embodied physical practice. At this stage, aikido was introduced not merely as a martial art but as a movement-based meditation, reinforcing flo , non-resistance, and bodily integration—all of which are central to transpersonal awareness.

A professional aikido instructor led the session, which lasted 30 minutes and was structured to mirror the mindfulness process—beginning with foundational alignment and body awareness before progressing into more fluid movement-based exercises

The specific training included

1.Foundational Aikido Postures and Movement Techniques

Participants were introduced to basic aikido stances, emphasizing natural alignment, stability, and breath awareness.

Initial drills focused on standing in a grounded yet fluid stance, with attention to balance and weight distribution.

Participants practiced rotational movements, fostering a sense of circular motion and redirection of force, a core principle of aikido.

2.Breath-Body Synchronization

Aikido emphasizes coordinated breath and movement, allowing for effortless execution of techniques.

Participants practiced inhaling during upward movements and exhaling during downward or grounding motions, reinforcing an integrated mind-body approach.

3.Partner Sensitivity Drills (if applicable within the session duration)

Some participants engaged in light partner exercises, exploring how energy is redirected rather than resisted—an essential aikido principle that aligns with transpersonal psychology's emphasis on ego-dissolution and interconnectivity.

After completing the aikido training, participants were given another 10-minute break to recover and reflect on the practice before progressing to the next phase of the study.

The integration of mindfulness meditation and aikido in this phase was not incidental—it was designed to be sequential, progressive, and interdependent. The meditation practice cultivated mental clarity, present-moment awareness, and emotional regulation, which were then carried into the aikido training, where they were translated into physical expression, movement fluidit , and embodied interaction.

Rather than treating these practices as separate techniques, this phase of the study emphasized their synergistic relationship, demonstrating how mental and physical awareness can be cultivated together. By structuring the training in this way, the research aimed to immerse participants in a deeply embodied experience, rather than merely having them execute predefined techniques

This comprehensive training process set the stage for the final performance assessment, where participants would apply their newfound awareness and embodied fluidity to acting, allowing the study to evaluate how transpersonal psychological training reshaped their artistic expression.

A professional aikido instructor led the session, which lasted 30 minutes and was structured to mirror the mindfulness process—beginning with foundational alignment and body awareness before progressing into more fluid movement-based exercises

1.After completing the aikido training, participants were given another 10-minute break to recover and reflect on the practice before progressing to the next phase of the study. The pose of aikido including standing naturally, standing around, and blowing in firm pose as the movements in Figure 1.

Figure 1 Sample movements of aikido

2. Footwork serves as the foundation of aikido practice, forming the basis for balance, fluidit , and coordinated movement. In this phase, participants were introduced to fundamental aikido footwork, emphasizing stability, weight distribution, and controlled movement. Unlike rigid, force-based stances found in some martial arts, aikido's footwork is rooted in natural positioning, promoting effortless redirection of energy and dynamic responsiveness.

Participants began by adopting a natural standing position, ensuring relaxed posture and even weight distribution. The training progressed systematically, focusing on three essential movement patterns:

1.Stepping Forward – Shifting body weight forward in a controlled and grounded manner.

2.Stepping Backward – Maintaining balance while retreating fluidl .

3.Side-Stepping – Engaging lateral movement to enhance adaptability and spatial awareness.

These movements were demonstrated in Figure 2, illustrating the correct sequence and alignment of the right and left leg movements. Under the guidance of aikido instructors, participants practiced these footwork techniques first individually before progressing to partner-based training.

Aikido is inherently relational, emphasizing interaction and harmony rather than isolated movements. As a result, this step required cooperative practice, necessitating at least two participants per exercise. The 40 participants were reorganized into 20 pairs, with each pair engaging in interactive footwork drills. This restructuring allowed for direct application of movement principles, as participants learned to adjust their stance, timing, and positioning in response to their training partner.

Under the supervision of aikido instructors, each participant took turns assuming the role of the initiator and the responder, mimicking the movement sequences illustrated in Figure 2. This approach not only reinforced technical precision but also fostered an experiential understanding of balance, resistance, and redirection—core principles of aikido that align closely with transpersonal psychological awareness.

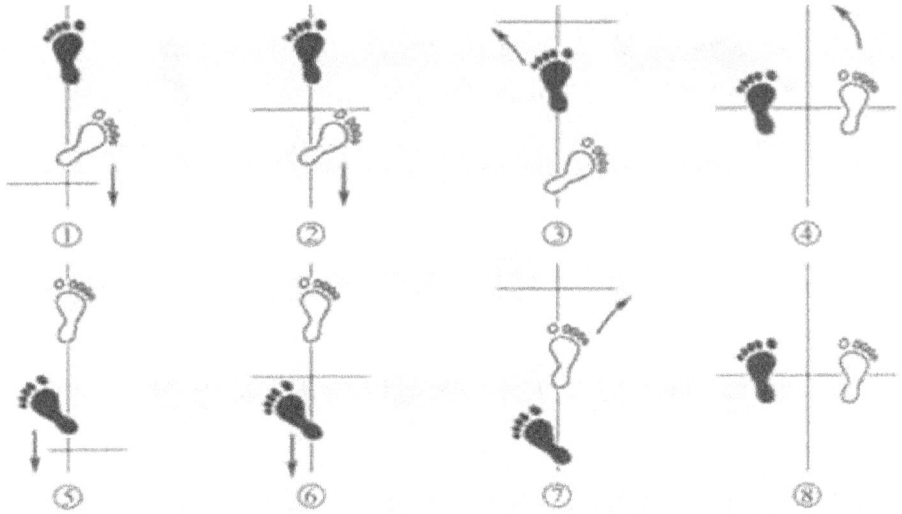

Figure 2 Sample movements for footwork

In this step, simple yet fundamental aikido movements were introduced to participants, focusing on the dynamics of attack and evasion. Unlike conventional martial arts, where combat often emphasizes forceful confrontation, aikido's philosophy revolves around harmonizing with an opponent's energy rather than opposing it directly. This practice was designed to allow participants to experience aikido's unique principles firsthand, shifting their perspective from aggression to cooperative movement.

Each pair of participants was assigned distinct roles:

One participant was given a wooden practice stick (bokken), symbolizing an attacking force.

The other participant remained unarmed, adopting the role of the defender.

The attacker's task was to execute controlled strikes toward their partner, simulating an offensive action. The defender's responsibility was to immediately evade the attack, utilizing fluid, circular movements to redirect energy rather than resist it. These evasive techniques—demonstrated in Figure 3—taught participants the importance of timing, awareness, and non-resistance.

Participants were instructed to repeat these movements in a continuous cycle, alternating roles after each sequence. This ensured that both individuals experienced both the attacking and defensive perspectives, deepening their embodied understanding of aikido's core principles. The ultimate objective was not merely to practice movement mechanics but to internalize aikido's emphasis on redirection, adaptability, and mutual responsiveness.

As the exercise progressed, participants were encouraged to shift their mental focus from the notion of combat to the experience of cooperative interaction. Rather than engaging in rigid, aggressive exchanges, they were guided to explore the subtle interplay of movement and energy, recognizing that aikido is fundamentally about flo , presence, and the dissolution of opposition.

By integrating these simple yet profound techniques, participants were not only learning physical aikido movements but were also developing a transpersonal awareness of relational dynamics, presence, and attunement to external forces—all of which would later translate into their performance practice.

Figure 3 Sample movements for quick runaround

By the conclusion of Step 2, all participants had completed the intervention phase, incorporating mindfulness meditation and aikido training into their experience. At this stage, participants were no longer engaging with acting solely through conventional performance tech-niques—they had now been immersed in transpersonal psychologi-cal practices designed to enhance awareness, presence, and embodied cognition.

From a transpersonal psychology perspective, this phase was more than just a training exercise; it represented a deep psychological and physiological shift. The intervention was not merely a technical addi-tion to their acting skills but a transformative process, shaping their ability to engage with their body, emotions, and presence in new ways. Having undergone this practice, participants were expected to enter the next phase of the experiment with heightened self-awareness, re-fined emotional control, and a deeper sense of embodied expression

Step 3: Second Drama Performance – Applying Transpersonal Psy-chological Training, In this step, participants returned to the stage for their second drama performance, allowing the study to evaluate the ef-fects of mindfulness meditation and aikido training on artistic expres-sion. Unlike the first performance, which was intended as a baseline assessment, this phase provided an opportunity to observe how tran-spersonal psychological interventions influenced acting performance in a real-world setting.

Each of the four contrast groups performed the first monologue of Juliet from Act III, Scene 2 of Romeo and Juliet (see Appendix B). This particular monologue was chosen for its rich emotional depth and nuanced expression, requiring actors to embody longing, internal conflict, and poetic sensitivity—elements that would reveal subtle yet profound shifts in their performance approach after the intervention.

Before stepping onto the stage, participants were given three hours of preparation time, mirroring the conditions of the first performance. This ensured that any differences observed in their acting could be attributed to the transpersonal intervention rather than additional practice time or familiarity with the material.

As in Step 1, the same audience evaluators assessed the performances, scoring each participant individually and independently using a structured evaluation score table (see Table 2). This controlled evaluation process allowed for a direct comparison between pre-intervention and post-intervention performances, revealing whether and how transpersonal psychological training had influenced the participants' expressive abilities.

Table 2 Evaluation Score Table after Transpersonal Psychological Practice

Participants No.	Group No.	Score (1-10)
01	1	XX
02	1	XX
...	...	...

In this final step, the evaluation score tables for all four participant groups were collected and analyzed separately. Given that each participant received scores from 10 audience evaluators for both the first and second performances, a structured and unbiased method was applied to calculate the final scores

To ensure fairness and minimize outlier influence, the final evaluation score for each participant was determined using the following procedure:

1.For each performance, the highest and lowest scores given by the evaluators were removed.

2. The remaining eight scores were summed, and the average score was calculated from these values.

3. This method ensured that extreme ratings did not disproportionately influence the final evaluation, enhancing the objectivity and reliability of the results.

The final performance scores of all participants, including their pre-intervention and post-intervention results, were compiled as shown in the sample format in Table 3. The actual performance scores and statistical analyses of the experiment are provided in Appendix C, where a comparative analysis of pre- and post-intervention performances explores the measurable impact of transpersonal psychological training on acting ability.

Table 3 Example of Evaluation Score of Participants

Participant No.	Group No.	Professional or not	First Performance	Second Performance	Result
01	1	Yes	2	5	+
02	1	Yes	3	6	+
...					

Step 4 (Continued): Interpretation of Performance Score Changes

In analyzing the evaluation scores, a notation system was used to categorize participants based on their performance improvement or decline:

1. "+" indicated that a participant received a higher score in the second performance compared to the first

2. "–" indicated that a participant received a lower score in the second performance compared to the first

This differentiation allowed for a clear, visual representation of whether and to what extent transpersonal psychological training influenced individual acting performance. By systematically applying this notation, the study could identify patterns of improvement, stagnation, or regression, offering deeper insights into how different participants responded to the intervention.

Step 5: Post-Performance Questionnaire on Transpersonal Psychological Influenc

Following the second performance, participants were required to complete a questionnaire (see Appendix E) designed to assess their subjective experiences and psychological transformation throughout the study. The questionnaire was developed based on theoretical foundations of transpersonal psychology, ensuring that the questions effectively captured key elements of transcendence, self-awareness, and embodied cognition.

The primary goal of the questionnaire was to distinguish between participants who experienced a strong intervention effect from those who were only slightly affected by the transpersonal psychological methods, including aikido and mindfulness meditation. To achieve this, the questionnaire used a structured response scale, in which:

Answers 3, 4, and 5 were classified as "positive responses", indicating that the participant had experienced a significant state of transcendence or heightened awareness due to the intervention.

Responses falling outside this range suggested a weaker or minimal effect from the transpersonal training.

Once completed, the questionnaires were collected and analyzed, allowing the study to explore the psychological dimensions of transpersonal intervention alongside the quantitative performance scores. By integrating objective performance data with subjective self-reports, the study aimed to present a holistic understanding of how transpersonal psychological methods influence both external artistic expression and internal personal experience.

Extracting Meaning from Experience

Evaluating Audience Reactions and Performer Feedback: To quantify the impact of transpersonal psychological interventions on acting performance, a binary scoring system was applied to the results from Table 2:

Participants who received a "+" (indicating a higher score in the second performance than in the first) were assigned a score of 1

Participants who received a "−" (indicating a lower score in the second performance) were assigned a score of 0.

For each of the four participant groups, the total number of participants who received a score of 1 was calculated. This figure was then converted into a percentage, representing the proportion of participants in each group whose performance improved following the transpersonal intervention.

The results of this analysis are presented in Table 4 and Table 5, providing a comparative overview of performance enhancement across the different experimental groups. These tables offer a structured, sta-

tistical representation of how mindfulness meditation and aikido training influenced acting performance across varying demographics and
experience levels, allowing for further interpretation and discussion in
subsequent analysis sections.

Table 4   Example Results of the Groups

Group No.	Quantity of participants	Quantity of "+"	Result
1	10	8	80%
2	10	6	60%
...	...	...	...

Table 5   Example results in the Group

Group No.	Senior learners in performance or not	Quantity of participants	Quantity of "+"	Result
1	Yes	5	4	80%
1	No	5	2	40%
...	...	...	...	...

In addition to analyzing overall performance trends, each experimental
group's data was further examined to assess how specific conditions
influenced participants' responses to transpersonal psychological interventions. For each group, the scores of participants under different
experimental conditions were collected and analyzed to determine the
percentage of participants who received a "+" within their respective
subgroup. This approach allowed for a more granular analysis, revealing whether certain participant characteristics (e.g., experience level,
gender, cultural background, or age) played a role in their responsive-

ness to aikido and mindfulness meditation training. For example, in Group 1 (Performance Experience Contrast Group), results indicated that senior learners in performance received a higher percentage of "+" scores compared to junior learners. This suggests that actors with more experience may have been better able to integrate transpersonal psychological techniques into their performances, potentially due to greater adaptability, enhanced cognitive flexibilit , or deeper emotional engagement. These findings, presented in the following tables, illustrate the proportional representation of participants who showed improvement ("+") relative to their subgroup total (five participants per condition per group). This structured analysis provides valuable insight into how different factors influence the effectiveness of transpersonal interventions in acting training, forming the basis for further discussion and interpretation in subsequent sections.

Interpreting Responses: Thematic Insights

In addition to performance evaluation scores, questionnaire responses were analyzed to assess the subjective experiences of participants following the transpersonal psychological interventions. The questionnaire was designed to measure the extent to which participants perceived changes in their awareness, emotional state, and embodied presence, which were influenced by aikido and mindfulness meditation practices.

Each participant's total questionnaire score was calculated based on their responses. The scoring system was structured as follows:

The lowest possible score was 10, indicating that the participant consistently selected "1" for all questions, suggesting minimal perceived impact from the intervention.

The highest possible score was 50, indicating that the participant consistently selected "5" for all questions, reflecting a strong perceived transformation due to the intervention.

By aggregating these scores across all participants in each experimental group, the study aimed to determine whether specific conditions (e.g., acting experience, gender, cultural background, or age) infl - enced the intensity of the perceived transpersonal experience.

The final results of the questionnaire analysis are presented in Table 6 and Table 7, providing a quantitative overview of subjective responses and enabling comparisons across participant groups. This data serves as a crucial supplement to the performance evaluation scores, offering a more comprehensive understanding of both the external artistic impact and the internal psychological effects of transpersonal training in acting.

Table 6 Example Result of Participants' Questionnaires

Participant No.	Group No.	Quantity of 3,4 or 5	Result
01	1	9	90%
02	1	6	60%
...	...	...	...

Table 7 Example results in the Group

Group No.	Senior learners in performance or not	Quantity of questions	Quantity of choice"3,4 or 5"	Result
1	Yes	50	40	80%
1	No	50	20	40%
...	...	...	...	...

The results of the questionnaire analysis were presented in terms of percentage values, representing the proportion of responses in which participants selected "3," "4," or "5" across the 10-question questionnaire. This approach provided a quantifiable measure of participants' subjective experiences, offering insights into the extent to which the transpersonal psychological interventions influenced their cognitive, emotional, and embodied awareness.

Furthermore, to refine the analysis, participants' responses were examined within their respective experimental conditions to assess potential differences between subgroups. This allowed for a comparative evaluation of how variables such as acting experience, gender, cultural background, and age influenced participants' engagement with mindfulness meditation and aikido training.

Each experimental condition consisted of five participants, and each participant responded to 10 questions, resulting in a total of 50 responses per subgroup. The final data were expressed as the percentage of total responses within the 50-question set where participants selected "3," "4," or "5", indicating a moderate to strong perceived impact of the intervention.

By structuring the results in this manner, the analysis provided a systematic comparison of subjective responses across different participant groups, facilitating a deeper understanding of how transpersonal psychological methods were experienced differently based on individual and demographic factors. The final results are displayed in the following table, offering a comprehensive overview of participants' reported psychological transformations.

Chapter 4:

Unveiling Patterns and Perspectives

Translating Experience into Understanding

A First Look at the Data:

How Performance is Perceived:Audience Perspectives: The data collected from the audience evaluations were systematically compiled
and analyzed, with detailed records provided in Appendix C. These
data offer direct insights into participants' performance progression
and can be summarized as follows:

1.Overall Performance Improvement

A total of 40 participants took part in the study.

29 participants (72.5%) received a "+", indicating that their second
performance demonstrated notable improvement compared to their
first

This suggests that, for the majority of participants, the transpersonal
psychological intervention—including aikido and mindfulness meditation—had a positive effect on their acting abilities.

2.Group 1: Performance Experience Contrast

This group consisted of 10 participants, with 5 senior learners (over three years of acting training) and 5 junior learners (less than one year of acting training).

8 out of 10 participants (80%) showed improvement in their second performance.

Among the senior learners, all 5 participants (100%) improved in their second performance, indicating significant adaptability and integration of transpersonal techniques into their craft.

Among the junior learners, 3 out of 5 participants (60%) showed improvement, suggesting that less experienced actors also benefited, though to a lesser degree.

These findings imply that while both senior and junior learners showed positive changes, experienced actors were able to integrate transpersonal psychological methods more effectively, possibly due to their existing acting skills and deeper awareness of performance techniques.

3.Group 2: Gender-Based Contrast

This group consisted of 5 male and 5 female participants.

8 out of 10 participants (80%) received a "+", demonstrating clear improvements in their acting performance after the intervention.

Among the female participants, all 5 (100%) improved in their second performance.

Among the male participants, 3 out of 5 (60%) showed improvement.

These results indicate that female participants appeared to integrate transpersonal psychological techniques more readily than their male counterparts. This could be linked to factors such as emotional expressiveness, openness to embodied practices, or differing approaches to performance engagement.

4.Group 3: Cultural Background Contrast

This group consisted of 5 participants from Eastern countries and 5 from Western countries.

7 out of 10 participants (70%) received a "+", indicating a strong effect of the intervention across cultural backgrounds.

Among the Eastern participants, all 5 (100%) demonstrated improved performance.

Among the Western participants, only 2 out of 5 (40%) showed improvement.

This suggests that actors from Eastern backgrounds may have been more receptive to the integration of transpersonal methods, possibly due to greater cultural familiarity with mindfulness and embodied movement practices. On the other hand, Western participants may have initially encountered conceptual or cognitive barriers in adapting to these methods but still showed positive outcomes.

5.Group 4: Age-Based Contrast

This group consisted of 5 participants aged 35-50 and 5 participants aged 20-35.

6 out of 10 participants (60%) received a "+", indicating performance improvement in the second session.

Among the older participants (35-50 years old), 4 out of 5 (80%) showed performance enhancement.

Among the younger participants (20-35 years old), only 2 out of 5 (40%) demonstrated improvement.

This suggests that more mature actors may have been better able to integrate mindfulness and aikido techniques into their craft, possibly due to greater life experience, deeper emotional engagement, and a more developed cognitive approach to acting. Conversely, younger actors may have struggled with the introspective and embodied aspects of the intervention, highlighting the potential for developmental differences in response to transpersonal training.

Key Insights and Interpretations

The findings suggest that transpersonal psychological training significantly enhanced acting performance across multiple demographic groups, though the degree of impact varied depending on experience level, gender, cultural background, and age.

More experienced actors demonstrated greater adaptability, possibly due to their established skills and ability to integrate new techniques into their performances.

Female participants showed higher improvement rates, suggesting a greater receptivity to transpersonal methods, which could be explored further in future research.

Eastern participants were more responsive to the training, which may reflect cultural familiarity with mindfulness-based and embodied practices.

Older participants exhibited more substantial improvements than younger ones, suggesting that emotional depth, introspection, and experience may play a role in the effectiveness of transpersonal interventions in acting.

These insights provide a deeper understanding of how actors engage with transpersonal psychology in performance training, emphasizing the potential for further exploration of its role in actor development and artistic expression.

Actor Reflections: The Inner and Outer Experience

The data collected from the questionnaire responses were compiled and analyzed systematically, with detailed records presented in Appendix C. These results provided direct insight into how participants experienced and internalized transpersonal psychological interventions.

Design and Interpretation of Questionnaire Responses

The questionnaire was explicitly designed to align with transpersonal psychological principles, assessing participants' self-reported experiences and cognitive-emotional shifts following the intervention. Each question offered five response options, three of which were categorized as positive indicators of transpersonal influence

"Confirmed

"Relatively Confirmed

"Highly Confirmed

Participants who selected any of these three positive responses were classified as having been notably influenced by transpersonal psychological methods, including aikido and mindfulness meditation. This classification allowed the study to distinguish between participants who experienced a strong psychological shift and those for whom the intervention had a lesser effect.

Findings from the Questionnaire Data

As shown in the tables in Appendix D, the questionnaire results were as follows:

A total of 40 participants completed the questionnaire.

30 participants (75%) selected "Confirmed," "Relatively Confirmed," or "Highly Confirmed" for their responses

This result indicates that 75% of participants demonstrated clear evidence of being influenced by the transpersonal intervention, supporting the hypothesis that aikido and mindfulness meditation had a measurable psychological impact on acting performance.

This finding is significant because it reinforces the effectiveness of transpersonal psychological training, providing empirical support that mindfulness and embodied movement practices can meaningfully shape actors' expressive and cognitive states. The consistency between the questionnaire responses and performance evaluation results further strengthens the reliability of the study's conclusions.

Validity of the Intervention and Statistical Considerations

The results suggest that participants who reported experiencing the effects of transpersonal training also exhibited observable performance improvements, aligning subjective self-reports with objective performance data. In this study, differences between experimental conditions were considered statistically significant if the variation between groups exceeded a margin of 5 participants. Given that 30 out of 40 participants (75%) self-reported significant influence, the findings suggest a strong correlation between transpersonal psychological practice and enhanced performance outcomes.

These results highlight the transformative potential of aikido and mindfulness meditation in actor training, emphasizing the role of transpersonal psychological methods in deepening artistic expression, emotional engagement, and cognitive flexibilit . By integrating both quantitative performance analysis and subjective experiential feedback, this study provides a comprehensive perspective on the impact of transpersonal psychology in performance-based disciplines.

What the Findings Reveal

The findings of this study provide compelling evidence that transpersonal psychological methods, including aikido and mindfulness meditation, had a measurable impact on acting performance. Through these interventions, actors demonstrated notable changes in their second performance, with the majority receiving higher evaluation scores from the audience compared to their first performance. This suggests that mindfulness and embodied movement practices contributed to a deepened artistic presence, enhanced emotional expressivity, and refined cognitive and physical coordination—all crucial elements in dramatic performance.

However, the degree of impact varied significantly across different actor characteristics, highlighting how experience, gender, cultural background, and age shaped the effectiveness of the intervention.

Acting Experience: Participants with greater professional experience in acting (senior learners) benefited more from the intervention compared to junior learners. Their performances showed a higher level of integration of mindfulness and embodied awareness, suggesting that experienced actors may have been better equipped to internalize and apply transpersonal techniques in their craft.

Gender: Female participants exhibited greater responsiveness to the intervention than male participants, suggesting possible differences in openness to embodied psychological practices or variations in emotional attunement.

Cultural Background: Actors from Eastern countries demonstrated a stronger impact from the intervention than those from Western countries, potentially reflecting cultural familiarity with meditative and movement-based disciplines.

Age Group: Participants aged 35–50 showed greater improvements than those aged 20–35, possibly due to a higher level of life experience, emotional depth, and cognitive maturity, which may have enhanced their receptivity to transpersonal methods.

Quantitative Differences Across Groups

The effectiveness of the intervention was further examined through quantitative analysis of questionnaire responses, where participants self-reported their subjective experience of the transpersonal psychological training. The total questionnaire scores, presented for each experimental group, illustrate the differential impact of the intervention across experience levels, gender, cultural backgrounds, and age ranges.

Group 1: Acting Experience Contrast

Senior learners (five participants): Total score = 40

Junior learners (five participants): Total score = 30

Difference = 10 points

This suggests that senior learners experienced a stronger integration of transpersonal psychological methods into their performance, likely due to their existing familiarity with performance techniques and ability to engage in deeper artistic embodiment.

Group 2: Gender-Based Contrast

Female participants (five participants): Total score = 35

Male participants (five participants): Total score = 23

Difference = 12 points

The notable gender-based discrepancy suggests that female participants may have been more attuned to the psychological and embodied aspects of transpersonal techniques, possibly due to a greater capacity for emotional openness or expressivity in performance.

Group 3: Cultural Background Contrast

Eastern participants (five participants): Total score = 39

Western participants (five participants): Total score = 28

Difference = 11 points

The stronger response among Eastern participants suggests that pre-existing cultural familiarity with mindfulness and embodied movement practices may have facilitated a deeper engagement with the intervention, whereas Western participants may have encountered greater conceptual barriers or unfamiliarity with transpersonal approaches.

Group 4: Age-Based Contrast

Participants aged 35–50 (five participants): Total score = 39

Participants aged 20–35 (five participants): Total score = 30

Difference = 9 points

The stronger response among older participants suggests that age-related factors such as cognitive maturity, life experience, and emotional depth may have contributed to a greater receptivity to transpersonal training, enhancing their ability to internalize and apply its principles in performance.

Key Takeaways and Broader Implications

These findings underscore the transformative potential of transpersonal psychological training in the performing arts, revealing its ability to enhance presence, embodiment, and emotional expressivity. However, the variation in impact across different actor characteristics suggests that the effectiveness of transpersonal interventions is influenced by personal, cultural, and developmental factors.

Experienced actors integrated transpersonal techniques more effectively, indicating that prior training in performance may serve as a facilitator for embodied awareness practices.

Female actors responded more strongly, suggesting that certain psychological and emotional dispositions may enhance receptivity to transpersonal methodologies.

Eastern participants exhibited greater responsiveness, reflecting the role of cultural background in shaping one's openness to embodied and meditative practices.

Older actors demonstrated more profound changes, suggesting that emotional and cognitive maturity may be key in absorbing transpersonal interventions in acting.

These results offer valuable insights for the application of transpersonal psychology in actor training, highlighting the potential for personalized approaches that account for individual differences. Future research could explore how transpersonal interventions might be tailored to optimize effectiveness across diverse populations, further expanding the integration of mindfulness and embodied awareness techniques in performance-based disciplines.

Demographic Considerations and Contextual Influence

Who Took Part in This Study? Before diving into the results, it's important to take a step back and look at who participated in this study. After all, when evaluating the effects of transpersonal psychological interventions on acting performance, understanding who these actors were, where they came from, and what shaped their backgrounds adds depth to the findings

This study was designed as a contrast experiment, involving two key groups:

1.Actors (Participants in the Experiment): The individuals whose performances were evaluated before and after transpersonal psychological training.

2.Audience Evaluators: The observers responsible for assessing performance quality and providing structured feedback.

In total, 50 individuals were involved—40 actors and 10 evaluators. Before any performances or interventions took place, all 50 individuals were asked to fill out a demographic information form, which provided valuable context for analyzing the impact of transpersonal training on different types of participants.

Who Were They? A Breakdown of Participants

Gender Balance:

20 participants (40%) were male

30 participants (60%) were female

Given the observed differences in how male and female actors responded to transpersonal interventions, this distinction was crucial. Would female actors, often thought to be more attuned to emotional and embodied practices, show a stronger response to mindfulness meditation and aikido? Would male participants, typically trained in more structured and technical performance methods, have a different learning curve? These were questions worth exploring.

Age Range:

38 participants (76%) were under the age of 35

12 participants (24%) were over the age of 35

The significance of this difference goes beyond mere numbers. Younger actors might bring energy, flexibilit , and adaptability, but would they struggle with the introspective depth required for mindfulness and aikido? Older participants, on the other hand, might possess greater emotional maturity and life experience, which could make them more receptive to transpersonal techniques. This study allowed for a comparative look at whether age influenced the ability to integrate these unconventional training methods into acting practice.

Cultural and Ethnic Background:

27 participants (54%) were from Western countries—including the United States, Canada, the United Kingdom, and Mexico.

23 participants (46%) were from Eastern countries—including China and South Korea.

This cultural mix was particularly intriguing. Mindfulness meditation and embodied movement disciplines like aikido have deep roots in Eastern philosophy, while Western performance traditions often emphasize psychological realism, verbal expression, and external technique. Would Eastern participants find aikido and meditation more intuitive, given their cultural backgrounds? Would Western participants approach these methods with skepticism, or would they ultimately embrace their benefits

Why Does This Matter?

Demographic information isn't just background noise—it's a key factor in how individuals respond to training, learn new techniques, and internalize artistic expression. This study wasn't just about whether transpersonal psychology works for actors; it was also about who benefits the most, how different backgrounds shape the experience, and what factors influence the depth of transformation

By considering these demographic variables, the study took on a richer, more complex dimension, allowing for a deeper understanding of how age, gender, and culture intersect with transpersonal psychological methods in the world of acting and performance.

Key Insights That Shape the Larger Narrative

This book explored the intersection of drama performance and transpersonal psychology, investigating how aikido and mindfulness meditation—two embodied practices rooted in heightened awareness and presence—could shape and enhance an actor's craft. Unlike conventional approaches to actor training that emphasize technical precision, psychological realism, or emotional recall, this study ventured into the transformative potential of mind-body integration, examining acting as a state of presence, flo , and attunement to the moment.

Through a series of contrast experiments conducted at Sofia University, the findings unfolded in two key dimensions

1.Transpersonal psychological methods, including aikido and mindfulness meditation, demonstrably influenced acting performance. Actors who underwent these interventions exhibited enhanced presence, emotional fluidit , and deeper embodiment of their roles, as reflected in audience evaluations and self-reported experiences.

2.Aikido and mindfulness meditation can serve as effective tools for actors seeking to refine their skills. Rather than merely being spiritual or meditative practices, these methods can be strategic performance enhancers, helping actors access a heightened state of flo , regulate emotions, and engage with their characters on a more profound level.

Yet, the influence of transpersonal psychology in acting was not uniform across all participants. Instead, individual differences played a significant role in shaping the extent of its impact

Experience Matters: More seasoned actors (senior learners) showed greater receptivity to aikido and mindfulness meditation than their junior counterparts. Their existing familiarity with performance training likely allowed them to integrate these new techniques more effectively, leading to deeper transformations in their craft.

Gender Differences Emerged: Female participants demonstrated a stronger response to transpersonal interventions, possibly due to higher emotional receptivity, embodied awareness, or intuitive engagement with mindfulness-based techniques. This raises fascinating questions about the intersection of gender, psychology, and acting methodologies.

Cultural Backgrounds Shaped the Experience: Actors from Eastern countries, where meditation and embodied practices are more deeply woven into cultural traditions, displayed a higher level of integration with these techniques. Western actors, more accustomed to performance training grounded in psychological realism and cognitive analysis, may have required more time to adapt to these unconventional methods.

Age Influenced Absorption: Participants aged 35–50 experienced a more pronounced effect from the interventions compared to those aged 20–35. The emotional depth, life experience, and cognitive maturity of older actors may have enhanced their ability to engage fully with transpersonal techniques, making them more receptive to the subtle nuances of aikido and mindfulness in performance.

Acting as a Transpersonal Practice: Beyond Technique: What emerges from these findings is a powerful insight: acting is not just about technique, emotional recall, or stagecraft—it is also a transpersonal experience, a state of deep presence where the actor dissolves into the role and the performance unfolds as an organic, embodied reality.

Through aikido, actors learned to move not from force, but from flow—engaging with their characters in a state of balance and redirection rather than resistance. Through mindfulness meditation, they cultivated a heightened sense of presence, allowing them to fully inhabit the moment rather than mechanically executing a script.

This book has demonstrated that transpersonal psychology has much to offer the world of acting, not as a replacement for traditional training but as a complementary approach that deepens an actor's connection to their craft, their body, and the present moment. By integrating aikido and mindfulness into their practice, actors are not just perfecting performances—they are transforming themselves in the process.

Acting, in its highest form, is not just imitation—it is presence. Not just performance—it is transformation. And transpersonal psychology may just be one of the most profound tools to unlock that transformation.

Chapter 5: Reflections and Implications

Tracing the Journey: A Synthesis of Key Insights

This book set out to explore an unconventional yet profoundly intriguing question: Can transpersonal psychology—through practices like aikido and mindfulness meditation—shape the way actors perform? Not merely as a theoretical concept, but as a tangible, experiential transformation that unfolds on stage?

Through carefully designed contrast experiments, actors engaged with aikido and mindfulness meditation as part of their performance training. The results were far from uniform—some found themselves stepping into a deeper state of presence and emotional fluency, while others experienced more subtle shifts. Yet, what became clear was this: transpersonal methods were not just passive exercises in relaxation, but active tools for shaping artistic expression.

Aikido and Mindfulness as Performance Catalysts

Both aikido and mindfulness meditation offered something beyond conventional acting techniques. Rather than focusing solely on emotional recall or external gestures, these methods encouraged actors to experience performance as a state of flow, presence, and deep attunement to their own bodies and emotions. Instead of performing a role, actors learned to inhabit it fully, accessing a kind of grounded intensity that felt more intuitive and alive.

Yet, not everyone responded in the same way. The depth of impact varied across experience level, gender, cultural background, and age, revealing fascinating insights into how different individuals absorbed and applied transpersonal training.

Who Experienced the Most Profound Shifts?

Experienced actors adapted more quickly. Senior learners—those with extensive performance backgrounds—showed a greater ability to integrate aikido and mindfulness into their craft, perhaps because they already possessed a heightened awareness of movement, rhythm, and emotional nuance. Junior learners, while benefiting, seemed to require more time to bridge the gap between traditional performance training and transpersonal methods.

Female actors exhibited stronger responses. The data suggested that female participants were more attuned to the intervention, responding with a heightened sense of embodiment and emotional depth. This raises interesting questions: Are women naturally more receptive to mind-body synchronization techniques? Or does traditional acting training differ in how it conditions men and women to engage with their physicality?

Cultural background played a role. Actors from Eastern countries—where mindfulness and embodied movement practices have a historical presence—seemed to incorporate these methods more intuitively than their Western counterparts. However, this did not mean that Western actors were resistant—rather, they approached the techniques differently, with some requiring more time to shift from analytical engagement to experiential immersion.

Older participants absorbed transpersonal methods more deeply. Those aged 35–50 seemed to experience a greater transformation in their acting process than younger participants. Perhaps life experience, emotional maturity, and a deeper sense of self-awareness played a role in this openness to new techniques. Younger actors, while certainly benefiting, appeared more focused on external performance execution rather than inner psychological shifts.

Acting as an Embodied, Transpersonal Experience

One of the most fascinating revelations was that acting—when approached through the lens of transpersonal psychology—was no longer just an external craft of mastering scripts, expressions, and gestures. Instead, it became an immersive, lived experience, where performance was something to be felt in the body, not just in the mind.

Aikido taught actors to move with their emotions rather than against them, to redirect tension rather than resist it, and to channel energy rather than control it. Mindfulness meditation cultivated a heightened awareness of presence, enabling actors to fully exist within a scene rather than mechanically perform it.

Through these insights, this book doesn't claim to offer a singular formula for artistic success. Rather, it invites actors, directors, and scholars to consider a different approach to performance—one that values presence over precision, authenticity over artifice, and embodiment over mere technique. Whether an actor seeks greater emotional depth, a more fluid connection to movement, or simply a way to access a deeper state of creative flow, transpersonal psychology may hold unexpected keys to unlocking new artistic possibilities.

Decoding the Findings: Layers of Meaning in the Results

What if acting wasn't just about memorizing lines, projecting emotion, or mastering stage presence? What if it was about something deeper—a way of being, a state of presence, an attunement to the moment that allows an actor to dissolve into the role completely? This book set out to explore that possibility through the lens of transpersonal psychology, using two unconventional training methods: aikido and mindfulness meditation.

The idea was simple yet profound: Could these transpersonal practices—traditionally used for cultivating self-awareness, flow, and non-resistance—help actors enhance their emotional expressivity, physical presence, and overall performance? Could aikido, with its emphasis on fluid movement and redirection of energy, teach actors how to embody their roles more naturally? Could mindfulness meditation, with its focus on awareness and presence, help actors stay fully engaged in the moment rather than getting lost in mechanical technique? The findings were as fascinating as they were revealing.

Actors as Living Instruments: Who Responded Best? Not all actors experienced the transpersonal interventions in the same way. Some felt an immediate transformation, while others required a longer period of adjustment. What made the difference? This study revealed that four key factors—experience, gender, cultural background, and age—played a major role in determining how actors absorbed and applied transpersonal techniques.

Experience Level: Seasoned actors, already familiar with the intricacies of performance, adapted more readily to aikido and mindfulness training. Their ability to integrate new techniques into their existing skill set allowed them to unlock a deeper, more embodied presence on stage. In contrast, junior actors, while still benefiting, seemed more focused on external technique and needed additional time to internalize these methods.

Gender Differences: Female actors responded more profoundly to transpersonal training, particularly in the areas of emotional receptivity and movement integration. Was this due to cultural conditioning, neurological differences, or training styles? The answer remains open to exploration, but the results suggest a potential link between gender and the ease of integrating embodied psychological techniques.

Cultural Influence: Actors from Eastern countries—where meditative and embodied movement practices have deeper cultural roots—showed a stronger response to transpersonal methods than their Western counterparts. This raised an interesting question: Do actors who come from traditions steeped in mindfulness naturally engage with these practices more intuitively? And, conversely, do Western actors, accustomed to more cognitive and externally focused acting techniques, require a different approach to integrating these methods?

Age and Psychological Readiness: Older actors (ages 35–50) exhibited a greater capacity for internalizing transpersonal techniques than younger actors (ages 20–35). This suggests that life experience, emotional maturity, and cognitive adaptability may enhance an actor's ability to engage with deep psychological and physical transformation. Younger actors, while certainly benefiting, appeared more concerned with technical execution and may have required a longer period of exposure to fully internalize the benefits of aikido and mindfulness.

Beyond Technique: The Actor as a Vessel for Presence: What these findings ultimately reveal is that acting is more than an external craft—it is an embodied state of presence. Many acting methods train performers to project emotion, control gestures, and manipulate their voices, but transpersonal techniques work differently: they train actors to inhabit the present moment, to let go of resistance, and to experience performance as a living, breathing phenomenon rather than a rehearsed sequence of actions.

Aikido teaches actors to move with energy rather than against it, to remain fluid in motion rather than rigid in control. It teaches them how to physically express emotion in an authentic, non-restrictive way.

Mindfulness meditation cultivates presence, emotional regulation, and deep listening. It enables actors to respond authentically in the moment rather than relying on pre-planned reactions.

This book does not claim that transpersonal psychology replaces traditional acting methods. Rather, it suggests that these ancient techniques offer something that many contemporary performance training programs overlook—an avenue for deeper psychological, physical, and emotional transformation.

Acting as a Transpersonal Practice: At its core, acting is about transcendence—the ability to step outside oneself and embody another reality with authenticity and depth. What this study has shown is that transpersonal psychology provides a powerful, tangible way for actors to access that state.

By integrating aikido and mindfulness meditation into actor training, we move beyond technique and into transformation—an approach that does not merely teach actors how to perform, but how to exist fully within the roles they inhabit. Acting, in its highest form, is not performance—it is presence. And transpersonal psychology may very well be the key to unlocking that presence.

Consciousness in Motion: The Expanding Dimensions of Experience

From the perspective of transpersonal psychology, consciousness is not a fixed or static entity but rather a dynamic, evolving phenomenon that exists across multiple dimensions. Unlike traditional psychological frameworks that often conceptualize consciousness as a linear or singular construct, transpersonal psychology emphasizes the fluidity, expansiveness, and transformative potential of human awareness.

The study of multi-dimensional consciousness is a fundamental aspect of transpersonal research, seeking to explore how individuals experience, expand, and transition through different states of awareness. Wilber (1975) introduced a hierarchical model of consciousness, proposing that human awareness unfolds through five distinct levels, each representing a progressive deepening of perception, self-awareness, and existential understanding (see Figure 5).

Wilber's framework offers a compelling lens through which to understand the transformative processes involved in acting, mindfulness, and embodied performance, as it suggests that consciousness is not merely a cognitive function but an evolving state that can be cultivated and refined through intentional practice. By engaging in techniques such as aikido and mindfulness meditation, actors may be able to access and navigate these levels of consciousness, deepening their connection to their roles, emotions, and the artistic process itself.

Understanding consciousness as multi-dimensional challenges the conventional notion that human awareness is a singular state. Instead, it invites a broader exploration of how transpersonal practices can serve as gateways to expanded states of being, ultimately influencing creativity, presence, and performance. The following sections will further examine how these dimensions manifest in both psychological theory and artistic practice, providing deeper insight into how consciousness shapes human experience and artistic expression.

THE SPECTRUM OF CONSCIOUSNESS

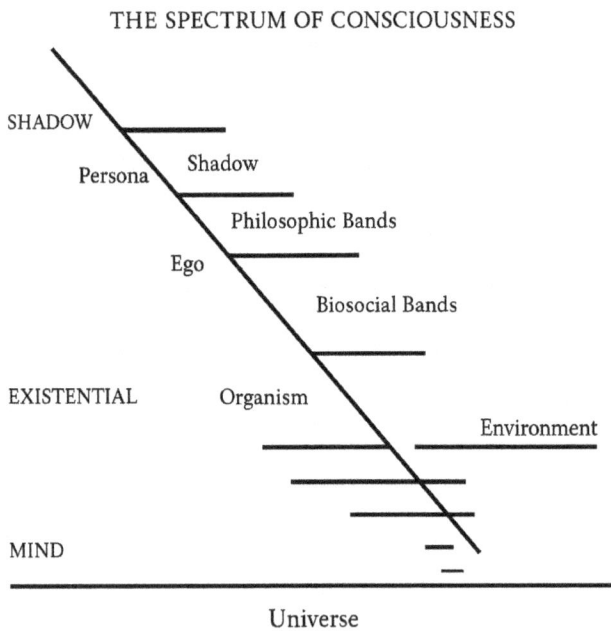

Figure 4: Prominent nodes in the Spectrum of Consciousness

What does it mean to step into a role? Is it merely an act of memorization and imitation, or is there something deeper—a transformation of consciousness, a shift in perception, a dissolution of boundaries between self and character?

In traditional acting methodologies, performers are often trained to craft a character from the outside in—adopting vocal inflections, physical gestures, and emotional cues that shape the illusion of another person. But what if acting were not just an external process but a multi-dimensional journey into self-awareness and transcendence?

From the perspective of transpersonal psychology, consciousness is not static—it is fluid, evolving, and layered. The process of embodying a role can serve as a gateway to expanded states of awareness, blurring the lines between self and other, mind and body, individual and environment.

This book explores how aikido and mindfulness meditation—two practices rooted in presence, flow, and non-resistance—can serve as transpersonal methods that facilitate the development of multi-dimensional consciousness in actors. Through experimental findings, it becomes clear that these practices do not merely improve performance technique; they reshape the way actors perceive themselves and their craft.

The Expansion of the Self in Performance: Ken Wilber (1975) proposed a multi-layered model of consciousness, in which awareness expands beyond the individual self toward an increasingly integrated and transpersonal perspective. This framework offers a fascinating lens through which to view an actor's journey:

1. The Role-Based Self – At this level, the "self" is diminished in favor of the "non-self"—the character being portrayed. The actor identifies

solely with the role, disconnecting from personal awareness and simply fulfilling an externally defined function.

2.The Private Self – Here, actors recognize their own inner experience but still perceive a separation between body and mind. There is an internal awareness, but it is compartmentalized, limiting the depth of emotional engagement.

3.The Integrated Self – At this stage, the barriers between body and mind dissolve, and the actor experiences a unified presence, where both physicality and psychology contribute holistically to performance. However, the environment is still perceived as external—something outside the actor's immediate sense of self.

4.The Transpersonal Self – This is the level where true transformation begins. The environment is no longer perceived as separate but rather as an extension of the self. The boundaries between actor, stage, audience, and character dissolve into a single, fluid reality. The performance is no longer something the actor "does"—it is something they "are."

5.The Universal Self – At the highest level, the self expands beyond individual identity, integrating fully with the collective, the universe, and the infinite. While rare in conventional acting, this is the kind of transcendence described in peak creative experiences—where the artist feels as though they have merged entirely with the performance itself, existing in pure flow, presence, and embodiment.

The findings of this study suggest that actors who engaged in aikido and mindfulness meditation showed measurable shifts toward higher levels of consciousness. These practices allowed them to navigate the self-role dynamic with greater fluidity, ultimately enhancing their ability to inhabit characters in a more profound and embodied way.

From Technique to Transformation: The Role of Transpersonal Practices in Acting

Before engaging with transpersonal psychological methods, many participants in this study experienced a rigid boundary between self and role. They approached performance as an external task, following a script and executing rehearsed expressions without a deeply integrated connection to character.

However, as the intervention progressed, participants began to experience a shift. Their awareness expanded, and the concept of "self" became less fixed and more permeable. Instead of merely performing a role, they began to experience it as an extension of their own consciousness.

By the time participants reached their second performance—after undergoing aikido and mindfulness meditation training—their self-awareness had deepened, their presence had strengthened, and their ability to merge with the character had transformed. They were no longer just "acting"—they were inhabiting a living reality.

These results align with Wilber's model of consciousness development, illustrating that self-awareness in performance is not a fixed trait but a state that can be expanded through transpersonal practice. The intervention functioned as a catalyst for personal and artistic transformation, pushing participants toward a more fluid and expansive sense of self.

The implications of these findings extend beyond individual performance training. They suggest that transpersonal psychology offers a valuable framework for understanding and cultivating artistic expression. As Scotton et al. (1996) noted, transpersonal psychology seeks to bridge the gap between body, mind, soul, and spirit, drawing upon a multi-disciplinary approach that integrates:

Biology and Neuroscience – Understanding the physiological impact of mindfulness and embodied movement practices.

Anthropology and Sociology – Exploring how different cultural traditions shape an actor's relationship with transpersonal experience.

Philosophy and Theology – Examining existential and spiritual dimensions of artistic expression.

Literature and Art – Investigating the ways transpersonal themes emerge in storytelling and creative works.

From this perspective, there is no single correct way to practice transpersonal psychology. Rather, any method that facilitates the transcendence of self-limiting consciousness can serve as a valid and meaningful practice. In this study, aikido and mindfulness meditation were used as transpersonal techniques, but the broader principle is that any practice capable of shifting an individual into an expanded state of awareness can serve as a tool for transformation.

Aikido and Mindfulness: More Than Just Training—A Way of Being

Aikido and mindfulness meditation were not chosen randomly for this study. Both practices share deep philosophical and psychological connections with the transpersonal experience. Aikido, originating from Japan, is unique among martial arts in that it emphasizes harmony over combat. Unlike other fighting techniques that focus on domination, aikido teaches practitioners to flow with their opponent's energy rather than resist it—a principle that translates powerfully into acting. Rather than forcing emotions or over-manipulating a role, actors trained in aikido learn to engage with their characters organically, responding fluidly rather than imposing control.

Mindfulness meditation, also rooted in Eastern traditions, cultivates heightened awareness, emotional regulation, and deep presence. It allows actors to inhabit the moment fully, silencing internal distractions and enabling a richer connection to character, audience, and environment.

Unlike boxing or wrestling, where the goal is to overpower an opponent, aikido and mindfulness focus on synchronization, energy redirection, and deep listening—all of which are invaluable skills for actors seeking greater authenticity and presence in their work.

Acting as a Path to Transcendence: At its core, acting is not just a technical craft—it is a process of transformation. An actor who merely executes rehearsed movements and scripted emotions may be technically proficient, but an actor who embodies their role as an extension of consciousness brings something much deeper—a presence that feels authentic, alive, and profoundly connected.

The results of this study suggest that transpersonal psychological practices—particularly aikido and mindfulness meditation—offer a pathway to that deeper state of performance. They enable actors to transcend egoic limitations, dissolve self-imposed barriers, and engage with their art as a living, breathing reality.

Ultimately, the study of transpersonal psychology in acting is not just about improving technique—it is about expanding the very nature of what it means to perform. By integrating transpersonal practices into actor training, we open new doors—not only for artistic expression but for the evolution of consciousness itself.

Meditation has long been regarded as a practice of stillness, introspection, and heightened awareness, yet in the realm of psychological research, it remains an evolving and deeply intriguing subject. Maslow once suggested that meditation was a field brimming with potential, an area still in its early but energetic stages of development. The growing body of research has provided compelling evidence of its effects—not only on psychological states but also on physiological and biochemical processes. Within the framework of transpersonal psychology, much of this research has been conducted under the umbrella of transcendental meditation, aiming to uncover the intricate connections between consciousness practices and scientific inquiry.

Baer (2003) distinguished between two primary dimensions of mindfulness meditation: one that assumes mindfulness to be an innate human capacity, where individual differences emerge from the varying degrees of natural awareness, and another that regards mindfulness as a trainable skill, something that can be refined and strengthened through structured practice. Depending on the intensity and duration of training, mindfulness meditation is further categorized into temporary practice, short-term training, and long-term training, each yielding distinctive psychological and physiological effects.

Empirical studies have consistently highlighted the transformative potential of mindfulness meditation. Short-term mindfulness training, for instance, has been shown to enhance self-awareness while simultaneously reducing emotional reactivity. Rosenberg (2015) examined the effects of mindfulness practice on individuals confronted with distressing imagery. The study revealed that participants who engaged in short-term mindfulness training reported experiencing heightened compassion in response to suffering while simultaneously displaying a significant reduction in emotions such as anger, contempt, and aversion. In other words, rather than resisting suffering or reacting defensively, these individuals exhibited greater openness and empathy. Farb (2010) took this exploration further by comparing neurological responses between a mindfulness-trained group and a control group. While both groups reported similar levels of sadness, the mindfulness group demonstrated increased activation in the right hemisphere of the brain, suggesting a fundamental shift in cognitive processing and emotional regulation. Such findings provide compelling evidence that even short-term mindfulness practice can lead to measurable changes in brain function, reducing susceptibility to unhealthy emotional responses.

Beyond its role in emotional regulation, mindfulness meditation also plays a crucial role in deepening self-knowledge. By cultivating focused attention and heightened awareness, individuals gain greater insight into their thoughts, behaviors, and emotional patterns. Through this process, meditation alters one's relationship with anxiety, shifting it from a state of external struggle to one of internal adjustment and acceptance.

Yet, while the psychological and physiological effects of mindfulness are increasingly well-documented, there remains an equally fascinating dimension—the role of culture in shaping the experience and effectiveness of transpersonal practices such as aikido and mindfulness meditation. The influence of cultural context in transpersonal psychology cannot be overlooked. Despite its Western academic origins, transpersonal psychology owes much of its development to Eastern traditions, including Confucianism, Daoism, Zen Buddhism, Indian philosophy, Islamic mysticism, and Japanese Shinto.

Eastern traditions, unlike early Western psychological models, placed a profound emphasis on spirituality, self-transcendence, and the interconnectedness of the individual with the universe. Central to these traditions was the notion of moving with, rather than against, the natural flow of existence—a belief reflected in concepts such as wu wei (effortless action) in Daoism, non-attachment in Buddhism, and the integration of heaven and humanity in Confucian thought. These perspectives introduced an entirely new way of approaching psychological inquiry, one that captivated Western scholars and ultimately played a pivotal role in the birth of transpersonal psychology.

One of the defining characteristics of transpersonal psychology is its ability to bridge mysticism and science. Whereas traditional psychological paradigms often dismiss or marginalize spiritual experiences, transpersonal psychology seeks not only to acknowledge but to integrate them into scientific discourse. It operates under the premise that spirituality, altered states of consciousness, and transcendent experiences are not mere anomalies but fundamental aspects of human psychology.

This fusion of Western scientific rigor and Eastern contemplative wisdom marks a significant paradigm shift. As Jung (1935) observed, the wisdom of ancient traditions should not be discarded in the pursuit of modern psychology, but rather integrated and refined. He argued that psychological growth and self-realization cannot be fully understood without considering the insights of cultures that have long explored the depths of consciousness. Jung's reflections underscore the profound and enduring influence of Eastern philosophy on the evolution of Western psychology, revealing that the intersection of these two intellectual traditions is not a collision but a convergence, a meeting point where science and spirituality inform and enrich one another.

Aikido and mindfulness meditation exemplify this synthesis. Unlike combat-oriented martial arts, aikido emphasizes harmony over aggression, redirection over confrontation. It teaches practitioners to flow with energy rather than resist it, mirroring many of the core principles found in transpersonal psychology. Similarly, mindfulness meditation shifts an individual's focus from reactivity to awareness, allowing emotions to be observed without attachment or resistance. Both practices cultivate a state of heightened presence, reinforcing the notion that true mastery—whether in martial arts, psychological growth, or artistic expression—is not about force or control, but about alignment, flow, and deepened perception.

This book does not claim that transpersonal psychology offers a definitive answer to the mysteries of consciousness, but it does propose a compelling way of thinking about human potential, performance, and self-realization. By examining the intersection of aikido, mindfulness meditation, and transpersonal psychology, it invites readers to reconsider how we understand personal transformation—not as a process of self-improvement, but as a journey of expanding awareness, dissolving barriers, and transcending perceived limitations.

The encounter between Eastern and Western cultures has not only shaped philosophical discourse but has also been a driving force behind the emergence of transpersonal psychology. The Eastern concept of the unity of heaven and humanity, which emphasizes the deep interconnectedness between individuals and the cosmos, has offered profound insights that influenced Western psychology's understanding of consciousness. Unlike the predominantly dualistic approach of traditional Western thought, which tends to separate the self from its surroundings, Eastern philosophy presents a model where the body, mind, and environment exist in harmonious integration. This shift in perspective has opened new pathways for exploring human consciousness, inspiring a psychological approach that does not merely analyze behavior but also acknowledges the transcendence of self and the potential for spiritual growth.

The application of aikido and mindfulness meditation in transpersonal psychology serves as a compelling example of this cultural synthesis. Aikido, originating from Japanese martial traditions, is not just a combat discipline but a practice deeply rooted in the philosophy of fluid motion, non-resistance, and the redirection of energy. It teaches practitioners to move with rather than against opposing forces, a principle that extends beyond physical movement into the realm of psychological flexibility, emotional regulation, and presence. Similarly, mindfulness meditation, which traces its origins to Buddhist contemplative practices, has been widely adopted in the West as a tool for self-awareness, emotional balance, and stress reduction. Together, these practices embody a holistic approach to self-transformation, offering actors and performers an opportunity to tap into deeper layers of presence, embodiment, and authenticity.

The findings of this book reveal that the impact of transpersonal psychological methods on performance is both profound and measurable. By engaging in aikido and mindfulness meditation, participants experienced noticeable shifts in their acting performances, which were assessed using two primary sources of evidence: the evaluation scores given by audience members and a structured questionnaire designed to assess participants' subjective experiences of transpersonal psychological effects. The data showed a consistent improvement in performance evaluations after the intervention, with actors demonstrating greater emotional depth, fluidity, and authenticity in their second performances.

These observations resonate strongly with Maslow's (1972) concept of transpersonal individuals—those who have undergone self-transcendent experiences and exhibit a heightened ability to perceive the world beyond surface reality. Maslow suggested that transpersonal individuals do not merely see objects for what they are but recognize their symbolic, sacred, and aesthetic dimensions. They are naturally inclined toward creativity, innovation, and a capacity to appreciate beauty in all aspects of life. More importantly, transpersonal individuals do not struggle with internal ambivalence; they express themselves with sincerity, emotional clarity, and an absence of psychological conflict.

This may explain why participants in the study achieved higher audience evaluations in their second performances. By immersing themselves in aikido and mindfulness meditation, they were able to transcend cognitive rigidity and engage more intuitively with their roles, allowing them to perform with a greater sense of presence and emotional truth. Rather than simply executing rehearsed lines and gestures, they seemed to embody their characters in a way that resonated deeply with audiences.

The questionnaire results further reinforce these findings. Participants overwhelmingly reported that they felt more attuned to their performances and experienced a shift in their state of consciousness during the second performance. Many selected responses such as "confirmed," "relatively confirmed," or "highly confirmed", indicating that they recognized the influence of transpersonal psychological methods in shaping their artistic expression. This suggests that the training did more than refine external performance techniques—it altered the way participants related to their own sense of self, role, and artistic process.

These findings have far-reaching implications beyond performance arts. They suggest that transpersonal psychology is not merely an abstract theoretical framework but a practical methodology that can be applied to real-world experiences, from creativity and self-expression to personal growth and emotional resilience. The fusion of Eastern contemplative practices with Western scientific inquiry provides an innovative lens through which human consciousness can be studied—not as a static entity but as an evolving, multi-layered phenomenon that can be cultivated, expanded, and refined.

This book does not claim that aikido and mindfulness meditation are the only pathways to artistic transformation. Rather, it proposes that transpersonal methods offer a powerful and underexplored dimension to performance training—one that allows actors to step beyond technique and into a state of heightened awareness, fluid embodiment, and deep psychological presence. In doing so, it invites further exploration into the role of consciousness in artistic expression, challenging conventional notions of acting as a purely technical skill and reframing it as a profound, integrative experience of self-discovery and transcendence.

From Discovery to Understanding: The Significance of Key Findings

Actors have long sought ways to deepen their connection to a role, to transcend the limitations of habitual movement and predictable emotional responses. In this exploration, the integration of mindfulness meditation and aikido practice offered a unique pathway—one that did not merely refine performance technique but shifted the very foundation of an actor's awareness, presence, and embodiment. These transpersonal methods, rooted in disciplines far removed from traditional acting training, provided a new lens through which actors could engage with their craft, allowing them to step beyond technique and into a more fluid, intuitive state of expression.

The sequence of these practices proved to be as important as the methods themselves. Actors first engaged in mindfulness meditation, which required stillness and an inward focus, before moving into aikido practice, which emphasized movement, energy redirection, and physical interaction. This intentional order ensured that meditation cultivated the actor's internal awareness before physical engagement took place, allowing them to enter aikido practice with a heightened sense of presence and receptivity. Had the sequence been reversed—had aikido preceded meditation—the physical demands of the practice may have left actors fatigued, disrupting their ability to enter the stillness required for meditation. Instead, the carefully structured approach allowed the mind to be prepared before the body was activated, fostering a harmonious integration of stillness and motion, receptivity and expression.

Beyond their individual contributions, the combination of aikido and mindfulness meditation proved more effective than either method alone. Movement-based practices, while invaluable for developing physical expressivity, often lack the deep introspective qualities that allow actors to connect with their roles on a profound level. Conversely, meditation alone, while fostering inner clarity, does not train the body to move with authenticity, fluidity, and presence in space. The integration of these two practices—one emphasizing internal awareness, the other external movement—offered a comprehensive approach to performance, allowing actors to bridge the psychological and the physical, the conscious and the subconscious.

What made this approach particularly compelling was the way it transformed the nature of performance itself. In their initial engagement with the script, actors approached their roles as a task to be completed, a structure to be followed. Their performances, though technically proficient, remained within the confines of learned behavior and preconditioned responses. However, after engaging with mindfulness and aikido, a fundamental shift occurred. The goal was no longer to act but rather to experience—to transcend the separation between performer and character, between movement and intention, between self and role.

The shift was not merely theoretical; it was observed and felt. Audience evaluations consistently reflected a deeper engagement, a heightened authenticity, and a more embodied presence in the second performances. The actors themselves, when asked to articulate their experience, overwhelmingly described a newfound ease, a reduction in self-conscious effort, and a greater connection to both their characters and their scene partners. More significantly, many struggled to pinpoint exactly what had changed—a testament to the subconscious nature of transpersonal transformation. Unlike traditional acting techniques, which often rely on deliberate adjustments and structured methodologies, the effects of transpersonal practice were felt rather than calculated, experienced rather than executed.

Perhaps the most fascinating aspect of this transformation was that actors entered the process without any preconception of what would occur. They were not attempting to improve their performances in a conventional sense; they were simply engaging in practices that cultivated awareness, presence, and flow. Yet, without consciously aiming for it, their performances improved in ways that transcended technical correction. They were not merely refining their skills—they were expanding their state of consciousness, removing internal barriers, and tapping into something beyond themselves.

Before engaging with these methods, actors relied on instinct and learned techniques, drawing from a familiar set of performance habits that, while effective, restricted their capacity for true spontaneity and depth. Without realizing it, they were limiting themselves to predictable interpretations, constrained by the boundaries of their own cognitive awareness. However, through transpersonal methods, something fundamentally different emerged—an approach to acting that was not about control, but about surrender; not about shaping a performance, but about allowing the performance to unfold naturally.

This experience raises intriguing questions about the future of actor training and the nature of artistic expression itself. If actors can achieve greater depth, presence, and authenticity not by working harder but by letting go, what does this suggest about the relationship between effort and creative excellence? How might performance training evolve if it were to focus not only on external technique but also on inner transformation?

The implications extend beyond acting. If mindfulness and aikido can alter an actor's ability to connect with a role, could similar practices reshape the way individuals engage with everyday life? Could the principles of flow, non-resistance, and deep awareness enhance not only performance on stage but also performance in interpersonal relationships, communication, and leadership? The results suggest that transpersonal psychology is not simply an academic or philosophical framework but a lived experience—one that can fundamentally alter the way individuals interact with themselves, others, and the world.

Ultimately, this exploration offers more than just a new approach to acting—it challenges conventional notions of selfhood, perception, and creative potential. It reveals that great performances are not crafted but discovered, that authenticity arises not through conscious effort but through a deep attunement to presence, and that the true power of performance may lie not in perfecting a role, but in transcending the boundaries of self altogether.

Actors often approach a role by drawing upon their previous performance experiences, using what they have learned from past roles to navigate new ones. This method, while seemingly logical, introduces a paradox: the more an actor relies on past experiences, the more likely they are to repeat familiar patterns, limiting their ability to engage with a role as something truly new. Every character an actor has played before leaves an imprint, shaping their understanding of who they are in performance. But what happens when an actor is confronted with a character that demands an entirely new approach—when the old frameworks no longer apply?

This challenge is deeply tied to the question of self-identity in acting. A performer may have once embodied the role of a teacher, only to find themselves now playing a student. While these roles appear distinct, the actor's instinct may be to anchor the new role in the old one, subconsciously blending past experiences with present requirements. However, acting demands a fluidity of identity, requiring performers to detach from preconceived notions of self and embrace a more malleable, adaptive presence. When this detachment does not occur, role confusion emerges, making it difficult for actors to inhabit their characters with authenticity.

One reason for this confusion lies in the way actors perceive the relationship between self and role. When performers approach acting as an external task, treating a role as an object to be molded rather than an experience to be inhabited, they risk becoming trapped within predefined character templates. Instead of discovering the role organically, they attempt to fit it into the framework of previous performances, leading to a rigid and often superficial interpretation. Over time, this reliance on past experiences creates a fragmented sense of self, where the actor struggles to separate their own identity from the accumulation of past roles.

This phenomenon is not exclusive to actors—it extends into everyday life. Individuals constantly shift between roles depending on their social contexts: a man may be a husband at home, a father with his child, a manager at work. However, when asked, "Who are you?", he is more likely to define himself by his profession rather than his familial roles. This selective self-identification reveals a cognitive bias—people tend to anchor their sense of self to the role they deem most significant in a given moment, often neglecting the broader spectrum of their identity. This limited self-definition can have profound psychological consequences: individuals who associate themselves with high-status roles may become overconfident and detached from vulnerability, while those who identify with perceived lower-status roles may experience self-doubt and diminished self-worth.

For actors, this misalignment between self and role can lead to performances that feel mechanical, unconvincing, or emotionally disconnected. When the self is rigidly defined by past roles, the actor's ability to explore new emotional landscapes becomes constrained. However, true artistry in acting requires the opposite—a state of openness, fluidity, and self-transcendence. The self must remain separate from the role, yet deeply engaged in the role-making process. This delicate balance allows actors to inhabit characters fully while maintaining the integrity of their own identity.

The process of acting, then, is not merely about learning lines or perfecting gestures—it is about navigating the space between self and role, about understanding the self not as a fixed entity, but as a fluid, evolving presence that can expand, contract, and transform. This process is, at its core, a transpersonal experience—one that transcends the ego's rigid definitions and allows actors to tap into a deeper, more authentic mode of being.

This research suggests that transpersonal psychological practices such as aikido and mindfulness meditation can facilitate this process, enabling actors to approach performance not as a series of techniques but as an exploration of consciousness itself. Aikido teaches the principle of flow—moving with rather than against energy—helping actors shed resistance and embrace movement with presence and ease. Mindfulness meditation cultivates self-awareness and emotional regulation, allowing actors to observe their impulses without attachment, to engage without becoming lost. Together, these practices offer a path to artistic freedom, empowering actors to break free from the constraints of past performances and engage with each role as a new, uncharted experience.

The findings of this book suggest that actors who engaged in transpersonal training exhibited a heightened ability to differentiate self from role. Instead of becoming emotionally entangled in their characters or repeating past patterns, they developed a more stable, expansive sense of identity. They no longer asked, "Is this me or the role?"—instead, they learned to navigate both simultaneously. In doing so, they achieved a level of psychological freedom that allowed them to fully inhabit the performance without losing themselves within it.

Emotional stability is a crucial aspect of this transformation. Acting often requires performers to access and regulate intense emotions, shifting between states of joy, sorrow, rage, and vulnerability with precision. Without emotional stability, these transitions can become psychologically taxing, leaving actors either emotionally drained or disconnected from the role. Transpersonal psychological methods appeared to help actors maintain a centered, grounded presence, allowing them to engage deeply without being overwhelmed by the experience.

Beyond emotional balance, these practices also appeared to enhance an actor's energy and stamina, a key factor in sustaining performance intensity. Many participants described a renewed sense of vitality after engaging in transpersonal training, reporting that they felt more present, more physically attuned, and more engaged with their roles. This suggests that aikido and mindfulness meditation may serve as tools not only for artistic development but also for psychological and physical well-being.

At its core, the process of transcendence in acting mirrors the process of transcendence in life. It is not about simply performing a role—it is about moving beyond habitual limitations, expanding awareness, and embracing new possibilities of self-expression. The findings indicate that actors who engaged in transpersonal practices did not simply improve their technical skills; they underwent a deeper transformation, shifting from "What I have" to "What I am", from "Becoming the role" to "Becoming more fully myself".

Ultimately, acting is more than a craft—it is a process of self-discovery and expansion. The goal is not to be a better performer but to be a more present, embodied, and authentic being. This is the essence of transpersonal psychology: a journey from identification to transcendence, from fixed self-concepts to an ever-evolving sense of presence. For actors, this shift is not just beneficial—it is essential. Only by breaking free from the rigid confines of past experiences can they step into the true depth and complexity of the roles they are meant to play—not just on stage, but in life itself.

The development of personality has long been a focal point in psychology, with scholars striving to understand the formation, evolution, and expression of self. Traditional psychological theories have sought to help individuals recognize their core personality traits, guiding them toward self-awareness and personal development. However, in the last few decades, the concept of sub-personality has gained traction, offering a more nuanced view of how individuals navigate multiple, sometimes conflicting, identities within themselves.

Personality is often thought of as a stable set of traits, including interests, motivations, skills, and behavioral tendencies. Yet, contrary to the assumption of rigidity, personality is fluid and adaptive, constantly evolving in response to age, experience, and environmental changes. What once seemed like an unchanging core identity is, in reality, a complex interplay of shifting perspectives and emergent traits. A person's motivations, desires, and abilities are not fixed; rather, they undergo continuous transformation, shaped by life experiences and shifting social contexts.

Much like the structural composition of biological and cosmic systems, the human psyche is multifaceted, comprising a network of sub-personalities—distinct but interconnected facets of the self that emerge in different contexts. These sub-personalities are often latent, surfacing only under specific conditions. For instance, an individual known for their rationality and discipline in professional settings may exhibit uninhibited emotional expression in moments of vulnerability. Similarly, someone labeled a "drunkard" in social settings may, in other domains, be an earnest lawyer, a dedicated teacher, or a disciplined athlete. The mistake, then, lies in overgeneralization—reducing a complex individual to a singular identity based on the most prominent sub-personality observed in a given moment.

Unlike core personality traits, sub-personalities operate with relative independence, coexisting within the individual while responding to external circumstances and internal conflicts. When faced with different social situations, competing sub-personalities may emerge, vying for dominance. The leading sub-personality at a given moment becomes the driving force behind an individual's actions, shaping their decisions, emotional responses, and interactions. This dynamic interplay between personality and sub-personalities introduces a critical distinction: while personality may shape an individual's general disposition, it is not synonymous with the true self.

In psychological inquiry, two levels of self-awareness must be considered. The first is the real self, which represents a deep, intrinsic sense of existence that transcends behavioral patterns. The second is the constructed self, composed of personality traits and sub-personalities—a collection of learned habits, behaviors, and skills that shift in response to external influences. From the perspective of personality psychology, these two levels operate on entirely different planes, and failing to distinguish between them can lead to identity confusion.

Within the context of performance, actors navigate both levels of self-awareness, drawing upon different aspects of their personality and sub-personalities in the process of role-making. In the first performance, before engaging in transpersonal psychological interventions, actors relied primarily on their pre-existing personality structures. Their roles were shaped by habitual tendencies, familiar expressions, and learned behavioral patterns, resulting in performances that mirrored aspects of their personal identity rather than fully embodying the character.

However, after engaging in transpersonal psychological practices such as aikido and mindfulness meditation, a noticeable shift occurred. The actors were no longer merely projecting their pre-existing selves onto the role; rather, they had begun to transcend the limitations of their habitual identity and engage with the performance from a more expansive, fluid state of awareness. The results of the questionnaire indicated that participants experienced a heightened sense of presence and engagement, suggesting that the intervention facilitated a deeper, more conscious interaction between self and role.

In this second performance, actors appeared to merge their sub-personalities with the demands of the role, rather than imposing a singular, fixed personality onto the character. Instead of being restricted by their personal traits, they were able to access different aspects of self, blending them in a way that felt organic and true to the dramatic context. This fluidity allowed for a more authentic embodiment of the role, as the actors no longer viewed the performance as a projection of past experience but as an opportunity to explore new dimensions of self-awareness and expression.

This transformation aligns with the fundamental principles of transpersonal psychology, which posits that the process of self-transcendence enables individuals to break free from habitual patterns and engage with experience in a more expansive, present, and integrated manner. Through mindfulness and aikido, actors were guided into a state where self-awareness and embodiment were no longer in conflict but in harmony, allowing them to move beyond personal limitations and fully inhabit the essence of their characters.

The influence of transpersonal practice extended beyond performance technique—it altered the way actors related to their own sense of self. The transition from "playing a role" to "becoming present within a role" marked a profound shift in conscious engagement with the performance process. This shift was not about learning a new acting technique but about experiencing a new way of being—one in which self-awareness, presence, and emotional authenticity converged to create a performance that felt both deeply personal and universally resonant.

Beyond acting, these findings have implications for broader psychological exploration. The realization that self is not a fixed entity but an evolving, dynamic phenomenon challenges traditional notions of identity, personal development, and emotional expression. If an individual can shift between different aspects of self within a performance, what does this reveal about the nature of identity in everyday life? If one can move beyond the habitual self to embody a more expansive awareness, could the same principles be applied to personal transformation, leadership, and emotional resilience?

Ultimately, this research highlights that acting is not simply an exercise in technical skill, but an exploration of consciousness itself. When actors engage in transpersonal practices, they are not merely refining their craft—they are stepping into a deeper state of self-awareness, a space where personality and sub-personality no longer confine expression but serve as vehicles for transcendence. The true power of performance, then, lies not in imitation, but in the ability to dissolve the boundaries between self and role, past and present, habitual and transcendent.

The effects of transpersonal psychological practice on actors' performances varied across different participants, influenced by their backgrounds, learning experiences, and individual conditions. The results of this exploration revealed two distinct phases: the first demonstrated the overall effectiveness of transpersonal psychological methods, while the second uncovered variations in impact based on participants' specific characteristics. This nuanced understanding suggests that transpersonal psychology is not a one-size-fits-all approach; rather, its influence is deeply intertwined with individual receptivity, professional experience, gender, cultural background, and age.

For actors with different levels of training, transpersonal psychological methods had varying degrees of influence. Those with more extensive experience in performance showed greater responsiveness to the interventions of aikido and mindfulness meditation. This raises an interesting point: professional training in acting does not necessarily diminish one's capacity for transpersonal intervention—in fact, it may enhance it. The structured training of experienced actors might serve as a foundation that allows them to integrate transpersonal insights more effectively, leading to a more profound transformation in their performances. Conversely, less experienced actors, while still benefiting from the intervention, displayed a comparatively smaller increase in audience evaluation scores. This distinction suggests that transpersonal psychological methods could be tailored differently for actors at different stages of their development—perhaps serving as an advanced technique for seasoned performers and as a foundational training tool for beginners.

Interestingly, the influence of transpersonal psychology was not only evident in actors' technical performance but also in their ability to embody emotional depth and presence on stage. The second performance, conducted after transpersonal training, demonstrated that actors became more attuned to the subtleties of their roles, exhibiting a fluidity and expressiveness that was absent in the first performance. This effect was particularly pronounced among those who had already undergone extensive professional training, suggesting that experienced actors may have a greater capacity to internalize the psychological principles underlying transpersonal practice.

Gender also emerged as a significant factor in how participants responded to transpersonal training. Female participants appeared to be more receptive to transpersonal psychological interventions than their male counterparts. This finding aligns with broader psychological research, which has suggested that women, on average, may display higher levels of emotional awareness, introspection, and receptivity to mindfulness-based interventions. The role of gender in the perception and internalization of transpersonal experiences has largely been underexplored in previous research, making this an important area for further investigation.

A possible explanation for this gender difference lies in the nature of aikido and mindfulness meditation as contemplative practices. Mindfulness meditation, in particular, is often associated with stillness, internal awareness, and deep self-reflection, qualities that some studies suggest women may naturally gravitate toward. Aikido, while more movement-oriented, is also fundamentally about harmony, yielding, and energy redirection, concepts that may resonate differently with

male and female participants based on cultural and physiological differences. While this does not suggest that male actors are less capable of benefiting from transpersonal psychology, it does indicate that
men and women may engage with these practices in distinct ways,
highlighting the need for gender-specific adaptations in transpersonal
psychological training for performers.

Beyond gender, cultural background played a crucial role in how actors
responded to transpersonal psychological methods. Participants from
Eastern countries exhibited a greater degree of receptivity to aikido
and mindfulness meditation compared to those from Western countries. This is perhaps unsurprising, given that both aikido and mindfulness meditation originate from Eastern philosophical traditions,
deeply rooted in concepts of non-attachment, self-transcendence, and
harmony between mind and body. Actors from Eastern cultures may
have already been culturally predisposed to the principles underlying
these practices, allowing them to integrate the techniques more seamlessly into their performances.

For participants from Western cultures, the philosophical underpinnings of transpersonal psychology may have presented a more unfa-
miliar paradigm. Western psychology has traditionally emphasized individual identity, cognitive control, and external expression, whereas
Eastern practices like mindfulness and aikido encourage inner awareness, surrender, and flow. As a result, Western participants may have
initially struggled with the abstract nature of transpersonal intervention, which could explain their comparatively lower receptivity to
the methods. However, the increase in performance evaluation scores
among Western participants after the intervention still indicates a tan-

gible, if less pronounced, impact.

Age was another factor that influenced the effectiveness of transpersonal psychological methods. Participants aged 35–50 showed greater responsiveness to transpersonal intervention compared to those aged 20–35. This may be due to life experience and cognitive maturity, as older participants may be more adept at integrating reflective, introspective practices. With age, individuals often develop a deeper understanding of self-transcendence, making them more open to transpersonal experiences. In contrast, younger participants—while still benefiting from the intervention—may have required more time and practice to fully internalize the effects.

These findings have profound implications not just for acting, but for the broader understanding of transpersonal psychology as a tool for creative and personal growth. By demonstrating that transpersonal practices can be adapted to different individual conditions, this book underscores the versatility of these methods. Transpersonal psychology does not offer a one-size-fits-all solution, but rather a flexible framework that can be modified to meet the needs of different learners.

This perspective also suggests that actors' training could be expanded beyond traditional technical exercises, incorporating transpersonal psychological methods as a core part of performance education. Acting, after all, is not just about memorizing lines and delivering them convincingly—it is about embodying presence, stepping into roles with authenticity, and experiencing the full range of human emotion without losing oneself in the process. Aikido and mindfulness meditation, by fostering greater emotional stability, self-awareness, and adaptability, can offer actors a powerful toolset to navigate the complexities of performance.

Moreover, transpersonal methods have the potential to help actors overcome psychological barriers. Many performers struggle with self-doubt, stage anxiety, or emotional detachment, challenges that cannot always be addressed through conventional acting training. By integrating transpersonal practices into actor education, performers could develop a deeper emotional resilience and a stronger connection to their craft. This would not only enhance performance quality but also improve the overall well-being of actors, reducing stress and fostering a healthier relationship with their art.

Ultimately, the findings of this book suggest that transpersonal psychology offers a valuable paradigm for actor training, one that bridges Eastern contemplative traditions with Western performance techniques. By incorporating mindfulness and aikido into performance practice, actors can develop a more profound sense of presence, enhance their ability to embody roles, and achieve greater psychological freedom on stage. While further exploration is needed to refine and adapt these methods, it is clear that transpersonal approaches have the potential to revolutionize performance training, offering new pathways for artistic and personal transformation.

For actors with different levels of experience in performance, the application of transpersonal psychological methods such as aikido and mindfulness meditation can be customized to suit their individual learning trajectories. Experienced actors, having already developed a solid foundation in performance techniques, may benefit from more intensified transpersonal training, allowing them to expand their expressive range and deepen their emotional connection to their roles.

For junior actors, on the other hand, a more gradual introduction to these methods may be necessary, ensuring that fundamental performance skills are developed alongside transpersonal awareness.

Similarly, gender differences may influence the effectiveness and reception of transpersonal psychological training. While both male and female actors exhibited improvements in their performances after practicing aikido and mindfulness meditation, the underlying mechanisms of transformation may differ. Psychological studies suggest that women may be more naturally attuned to introspective and contemplative practices, whereas men may respond more readily to physical, movement-based interventions. With this in mind, transpersonal psychological training for actors could be tailored to leverage these natural inclinations, incorporating a balance between stillness and movement, introspection and action, discipline and surrender.

Geographic and cultural background also played a role in shaping the effectiveness of transpersonal interventions. Actors from Eastern cultures, where mindfulness and aikido originated, appeared to internalize these practices with greater ease, suggesting that familiarity with certain philosophical and spiritual traditions might enhance receptivity to transpersonal techniques. Conversely, actors from Western cultures, who may be more accustomed to psychological frameworks emphasizing cognitive control and individual identity, may require a different pedagogical approach, one that introduces transpersonal principles in a way that aligns with their existing worldview.

Age also emerged as a factor influencing the depth of engagement with transpersonal training. Younger actors, particularly those aged 20–35, may benefit from an intensified approach, as they may still be developing the cognitive and emotional maturity necessary for deeper transpersonal insights. Meanwhile, older actors—with a broader life experience and possibly a greater openness to introspective practices—may find themselves more naturally inclined to the principles of transpersonal psychology, allowing for a more immediate and profound integration of these techniques into their performance practice.

Maslow's distinction between healthy self-actualization and transpersonal self-actualization provides an important framework for understanding these findings. Healthy self-actualization, in Maslow's terms, refers to the individual's fulfillment of their personal potential, a process that involves self-discovery, the pursuit of intrinsic motivations, and a harmonious alignment with one's inner nature. However, transpersonal self-actualization goes beyond personal fulfillment—it represents a state of transcendence, in which individuals become fully immersed in experiences that extend beyond the self, often experiencing moments of peak consciousness that dissolve personal boundaries and create a sense of oneness with life and the universe.

Maslow (1972) further explored the characteristics of individuals who had reached a state of self-transcendence, noting that these individuals possessed an innate fluency in the "language of being"—a way of perceiving and expressing reality that was deeply intuitive, creative, and symbolic. According to Maslow, transcendent individuals effortlessly interpret and communicate through metaphors, paradoxes, art, music, and other non-verbal modes of expression, understanding the interconnectedness of all things and navigating the world with a heightened sense of purpose and clarity.

In this study, participants who engaged in aikido and mindfulness meditation exhibited signs of this transpersonal shift. The intervention appeared to activate latent capacities for intuitive expression, allowing actors to approach their performances with a newfound depth and authenticity. This suggests that aikido and mindfulness meditation may serve as catalysts for self-transcendence, helping actors not only refine their technical craft but also access higher states of consciousness that enhance their artistic and personal development.

Furthermore, the concept of peak experiences—a key component of transpersonal psychology—provides another lens through which to understand the improvement in actors' performances. Peak experiences, as described by Maslow, are moments of profound joy, clarity, and self-transcendence, where individuals feel fully present, deeply connected, and effortlessly expressive. These moments often coincide with artistic breakthroughs, allowing performers to tap into a heightened state of flow where creativity and authenticity emerge effortlessly.

Actors who engaged in transpersonal training reported a heightened sense of presence, emotional depth, and connectedness to their roles, suggesting that they may have experienced micro-versions of peak experiences during their second performances. This would help explain why their performances improved so significantly—not just in technical skill, but in expressive authenticity and emotional resonance.

Ultimately, this study suggests that transpersonal psychological methods—including aikido and mindfulness meditation—offer a powerful gateway into self-transcendence for actors. By guiding performers into a state of expanded consciousness, these practices appear to facilitate a deeper engagement with both the self and the role being portrayed.

The implications extend beyond acting—if transpersonal techniques can enhance creativity, emotional intelligence, and presence, could they also be applied to other domains of human experience, from leadership and education to therapy and personal transformation?

While further research is needed to refine and expand upon these findings, one thing is clear: acting is more than a craft—it is a form of self-exploration and transformation. When actors engage with their work from a transpersonal perspective, they do not simply perform—they become conduits for something greater, embodying a state of presence and authenticity that resonates beyond the stage.

Bridging Theory and Practice: Transformative Applications

Currently, the teaching and learning of performance primarily rely on theoretical instruction and practical training derived from professional educational materials. Aspiring actors acquire technical skills and theoretical knowledge from structured curricula and refine their craft under the guidance of experienced instructors. Among the various branches of performing arts education, drama performance occupies a distinct and significant position, distinguished from other performance forms by its unique demands on both the body and the psyche. Unlike other forms of artistic expression, drama requires actors to overcome psychological and physical barriers, as their state of mind and body directly influences their ability to fully embody a role. The challenge is heightened by the constraints of time, space, and the immediate nature of live performance, where actors must seamlessly transition into character within a specific setting and a finite timeframe.

This study has provided insightful evidence on the impact of transpersonal psychology on drama performance, offering valuable implications for both acting pedagogy and professional training. The findings suggest that transpersonal psychological techniques, such as aikido and mindfulness meditation, may enhance actors' ability to achieve an optimal mental state for performance, equipping them with tools to navigate emotional and physical challenges, manage role conflicts, and refine their craft at a deeper level. These methods do not merely enhance performance technique—they facilitate a profound exploration of selfhood, enabling actors to transcend personal limitations and immerse themselves in their roles with heightened awareness and presence.

A key revelation of this research is that actors who engage in transpersonal psychological practices experience an enhanced ability to access the "real self," a crucial element in achieving authenticity in performance. The journey of self-transcendence, facilitated through techniques like aikido and mindfulness meditation, allows performers to redefine their relationship with the roles they inhabit. Instead of merely projecting learned behaviors and mimetic expressions, actors internalize a role in a way that bridges personal identity with artistic interpretation, resulting in a more genuine and immersive performance.

Moreover, this study highlights how individual differences—such as prior experience, gender, age, and cultural background—affect the extent to which actors respond to transpersonal psychological methods. The evidence suggests that actors with varying learning conditions and personal attributes require tailored transpersonal approaches to optimize their engagement with performance training.

For instance, female actors in this study demonstrated a greater receptivity to transpersonal psychological interventions compared to their male counterparts. This suggests that men may require a modified or intensified approach in order to achieve a comparable level of engagement. If transpersonal methods are to be integrated into performance training on a broader scale, instructors may need to adjust the intensity and structure of these practices to account for individual variations.

Such insights hold profound implications for drama education and professional actor training. Traditionally, performance pedagogy has focused predominantly on technical mastery, character development, and interpretative skills, often neglecting the deeper psychological and emotional processes that underpin an actor's ability to fully inhabit a role. By integrating transpersonal techniques into drama education, training programs can equip actors with the tools to navigate the complexities of role immersion, emotional authenticity, and sustained stage presence.

In essence, this study presents a compelling argument for rethinking traditional approaches to acting pedagogy. The incorporation of transpersonal psychological methods into performance training has the potential to revolutionize the way actors engage with their craft, offering a pathway toward greater artistic depth, psychological resilience, and self-awareness. By harnessing the transformative potential of practices like aikido and mindfulness meditation, actors can achieve a heightened state of presence, emotional intelligence, and creative fluency, ultimately enriching both their performances and their personal growth as artists.

Navigating the Boundaries: Challenges and Considerations

While this book has illuminated the profound effects of transpersonal psychological methods on drama performance, it is essential to acknowledge the nuances and complexities that come with exploring the intersection of psychology and artistic expression. No research or exploration—no matter how comprehensive—captures the full picture, and it is in these gaps that future discoveries and refinements emerge.

One of the key areas for further inquiry lies in the diversity of participants. Every actor comes to the stage carrying a unique combination of training, personal experience, and cultural background, all of which shape how they respond to transpersonal practices like aikido and mindfulness meditation. While this book has shown that these methods enhance presence, emotional depth, and role embodiment, the variations in individual receptivity suggest that different actors may require different approaches. Future explorations might look at how actors from distinct theatrical traditions—whether method acting, classical training, or physical theater—experience and integrate transpersonal psychological techniques into their craft.

The duration of practice is another factor worth reconsidering. The aikido and mindfulness interventions in this study were applied over a limited period, yielding immediate and tangible improvements in performance. But what happens when an actor engages with these practices over years rather than weeks? Would their ability to access states of flow, heightened awareness, and emotional authenticity become second nature? Would their relationship with the craft itself transform? These are questions that demand further exploration, perhaps through longitudinal studies tracking actors who integrate transpersonal training into their careers over time.

Another intriguing dimension is the subjectivity of performance evaluation. While audience feedback and self-reported experiences provided compelling insights, performance is not an easily quantifiable phenomenon. What one viewer finds deeply moving, another might find unremarkable. Future studies might incorporate neurological or physiological markers—such as changes in heart rate variability or brainwave patterns—to examine the actor's psychological state during performance. Imagine being able to observe, in real time, how an actor's consciousness shifts as they step into a role, moving between different states of self-awareness and artistic immersion. Such findings could provide scientific validation for what actors and performers have long known intuitively—that great performance is not just about technique but about the alchemy of mind, body, and presence.

Beyond the individual actor, a larger question remains: What happens when transpersonal psychological methods are applied to an entire ensemble? Theater, after all, is a collective act, a conversation between actors, audience, and text. If one actor benefits from aikido and mindfulness, how might an entire cast, trained in these methods, generate a deeper sense of ensemble cohesion, intuitive interplay, and shared presence on stage? Would performances become more fluid, more organic, more alive? Would actors find themselves tuning into each other on a level beyond spoken words and scripted interactions? This is an exciting avenue for further exploration—one that could redefine not just individual performance but the dynamics of theatrical collaboration itself.

Then, of course, there is the question of other transpersonal techniques. While aikido and mindfulness meditation proved to be highly effective in unlocking deeper dimensions of presence and embodiment, they are by no means the only tools available. What about breathwork, ecstatic dance, visualization practices, or dream work? Could lucid dreaming, for example, allow actors to rehearse their roles in subconscious states, making their performances even more intuitive and embodied? Could practices drawn from shamanic traditions—ritual movement, deep trance states—further expand the actor's capacity to dissolve into a role?

Ultimately, what this book has shown is not merely that transpersonal psychological methods enhance performance, but that they open the door to an entirely new way of thinking about acting. The craft of performance is often framed as a set of external techniques—voice control, physical movement, script analysis—but what if it is just as much about internal expansion, states of awareness, and self-transcendence? What if the greatest performances are not just the result of skill but of an altered relationship with self, role, and reality?

These questions remain open, and that is precisely what makes this journey so exhilarating. Performance is, at its core, an exploration of what it means to be human—to step into another's skin, to embody experiences beyond one's own, to channel emotions and stories that resonate across time and space. Transpersonal psychology offers a way of deepening this exploration, not just as a tool for acting, but as a gateway to a more profound engagement with the world, the self, and the shared human experience.

And so, rather than a conclusion, this book leaves you with an invitation—to continue the exploration, to experiment with transpersonal practices in your own creative work, and to consider how the boundaries between performance, self, and consciousness are far more fluid than we often assume. In the end, perhaps the stage is not just a platform for acting, but a mirror for transformation, reflecting back the infinite possibilities of what it means to be alive.

Representation and Diversity: Reflections on the Study Sample

As with any exploration of human experience, the diversity and representation of the study sample play a crucial role in shaping the findings. While this study has provided valuable insights into the effects of transpersonal psychological methods on acting performance, it is important to acknowledge that the relatively limited sample size presents certain constraints. Would the results hold if the study were expanded? Would a larger, more diverse pool of participants yield deeper, more nuanced findings? These are essential questions for future exploration.

One of the ongoing debates in psychological and performance studies is the optimal number of participants required to generate reliable and meaningful conclusions. While smaller sample sizes allow for more in-depth, qualitative analysis, larger groups could provide broader statistical validation, revealing patterns and underlying principles that might not be as apparent in a more limited study. If transpersonal psychological methods are to be integrated into mainstream acting training, larger-scale studies will be essential—not only to confirm the trends observed here but also to fine-tune how these techniques can be adapted for different individuals, cultures, and performance styles.

In future research, expanding the number of participants across all contrast groups would offer a more comprehensive understanding of how various factors—such as prior acting experience, cultural background, age, and gender—interact with transpersonal psychological interventions. For instance, would a larger sample reinforce the idea that senior actors benefit more from transpersonal methods, or would new patterns emerge? Would cultural differences remain as pronounced, or would additional variables, such as personal openness to meditative and movement-based practices, prove to be even more significant?

Beyond just increasing numbers, diversity within the participant pool is another crucial consideration. While this study included actors from different cultural backgrounds, age groups, and levels of experience, a broader selection could further illuminate how individual differences shape the effectiveness of transpersonal techniques. Future research could explore actors from a wider range of theatrical traditions, comparing, for example, the effects of transpersonal training on method actors versus those trained in classical Shakespearean techniques or contemporary experimental theater.

Moreover, incorporating actors from different performance mediums—such as film, television, and improvisational theater—could reveal how transpersonal psychology influences presence, adaptability, and spontaneity in various artistic contexts. Would actors trained in screen acting, who often work in fragmented, highly technical shooting environments, experience the same benefits from aikido and mindfulness as those performing in live theater, where presence and physicality are emphasized? These are critical questions that future research could address, potentially broadening the impact of transpersonal psychology beyond the stage and into the larger realm of creative expression.

While this study serves as a foundational step in understanding the role of transpersonal psychological methods in acting, it is by no means the final word. The findings invite further experimentation, refinement, and expansion, not only to strengthen the evidence base but also to ensure that the insights gained can be applied in diverse and inclusive ways. By continuing to explore how transpersonal techniques interact with different artistic traditions, cultural perspectives, and individual psychologies, future research can further unveil the transformative power of these methods, potentially reshaping the way actors train, perform, and experience their craft.

Theatrical Choices and Their Influence on Interpretation

The selection of dramatic material plays a pivotal role in shaping an actor's performance and the audience's perception. No script exists in isolation—it carries with it a history of interpretation, a legacy of past performances, and often, a set of implicit expectations about who should play a given role. This study's approach to performance experimentation, while illuminating in many respects, inevitably encountered certain limitations related to role suitability and audience perception.

Consider, for instance, the expectation of age, gender, or physicality in a role. If a twenty-year-old male protagonist has historically been played by young male actors, placing a forty-year-old female performer in the same role might create a disconnect for audiences accustomed to traditional casting norms. While in some cases, such unconventional casting can lead to fresh, compelling reinterpretations, in an experimental setting where performance is being evaluated in a structured manner, such discrepancies could introduce biases that have nothing to do with the effectiveness of the actor's craft. This raises a crucial question—how much does the audience's perception of a role depend on the actor's alignment with expected characteristics, and how much is truly influenced by the depth and authenticity of performance itself?

Theater, as an art form, has long grappled with the balance between tradition and innovation. On the one hand, classical roles have been performed for centuries with specific conventions, with rigid expectations regarding gender, age, and even physical appearance. On the other hand, experimental theater, contemporary reimaginings, and non-traditional casting have proven that great performances transcend these constraints. A powerful interpretation of a role can challenge preconceived notions, alter an audience's emotional response, and redefine a character's meaning in unexpected ways.

That being said, when evaluating the effectiveness of transpersonal psychological methods in performance training, it is crucial to ensure that actors are working with material that allows them to fully explore and express their abilities, rather than being constrained by elements beyond their control. If an actor's score from the audience is influenced not by their performance quality but by pre-existing expectations about the character, then the study's conclusions become less about the effectiveness of transpersonal interventions and more about the biases inherent in theatrical tradition.

A more scientific and equitable approach to performance-based experimentation might involve matching actors with roles that align more closely with their personal characteristics, or, alternatively, ensuring that the audience is aware in advance that the casting is deliberately non-traditional, allowing them to focus on the actor's interpretative depth rather than surface-level alignment with a prototype. Future research might also explore whether actors who have undergone transpersonal psychological training are better able to transcend these audience biases, immersing themselves so deeply in their roles that traditional expectations dissolve in favor of a more profound engagement with the character's essence.

This raises a fascinating artistic question: How much of an actor's success is dictated by external perception, and how much is truly within their control? If transpersonal methods can equip performers with a stronger sense of self-transcendence, heightened awareness, and emotional fluidity, might they be able to break through conventional barriers of typecasting, physical expectations, and rigid role definitions?

Looking ahead, the rigid assignment of dramatic material to all actors in an experiment may not be necessary. Instead, actors could be given roles that suit their personal attributes, or, alternatively, placed in non-traditional casting scenarios with a specific emphasis on evaluating how well they embody the essence of a character beyond surface-level expectations. A more flexible and actor-centered approach to role selection could ensure that the evaluation of performance remains focused on the quality of craft rather than the constraints of tradition.

Ultimately, theater thrives on reinvention, and the findings from this study open a broader dialogue on how transpersonal psychological techniques might not only enhance an actor's internal process but also equip them with the tools to navigate and challenge external biases in the theatrical world. The question is not just how well an actor fits a role—but how deeply they can inhabit it, transform it, and make it their own.

Beyond the Present: Pathways for Future Inquiry

This book has explored the profound intersection between performance and transpersonal psychology, shedding light on the ways in which aikido and mindfulness meditation can enhance the actor's craft. Yet, as with any compelling inquiry, the real journey does not end here—it extends into the unknown, the experimental, and the yet-to-be-discovered. The stage, as it were, is set for something even greater: the practical application of these insights into the very fabric of performance training.

Imagine a future where actor training does not simply focus on technical mastery—voice projection, movement, and emotional recall—but also cultivates an actor's ability to enter altered states of consciousness, heighten self-awareness, and transcend their own habitual patterns of thinking and feeling. What if drama schools incorporated aikido and mindfulness not just as peripheral exercises but as core elements of actor training, shaping how performers inhabit their roles, interact with fellow actors, and engage with an audience on a deeply intuitive level?

The implications of this work stretch far beyond the scope of individual performance improvement. Could transpersonal methods redefine the way theater itself is created? If actors were trained in a state of heightened awareness, could entire productions take on a more fluid, improvisational quality, where presence, intuition, and deep listening become the foundations of storytelling? Could directors develop new methodologies based on the principles of aikido—blending with the energy of the scene rather than forcing it—resulting in performances that are more dynamic and alive?

These are not just hypothetical questions. They are invitations—to researchers, actors, educators, and practitioners alike—to experiment, challenge, and expand upon these findings. Future studies will be tasked with translating these principles into practical, repeatable techniques that can be used in performance training. This might involve structured curricula, where actors undergo immersive training in transpersonal psychological techniques before stepping into the rehearsal room. It could also involve longitudinal studies, where performers are observed over years to determine the lasting effects of these methods on their craft.

But there is also room for the unexpected, the unconventional, and the radical. Could transpersonal psychology be applied beyond traditional theater spaces? Imagine performances where the audience, too, is invited into a transpersonal experience, where theater is no longer about passive spectatorship but about shared states of consciousness, collective immersion, and energetic exchange between performer and observer. Could performance itself become a transformative ritual, dissolving the boundaries between actor and audience, self and role, consciousness and embodiment?

Perhaps the most important realization from this exploration is that transpersonal psychology is not merely a tool for improving acting—it is a philosophy, a way of approaching performance (and perhaps life itself) with a deeper sense of awareness, flow, and interconnectedness. The journey does not end here; it only widens, inviting new perspectives, new voices, and new possibilities.

And so, the question remains: What comes next? If performance is a reflection of the human experience, and transpersonal psychology is a pathway to deeper understanding, then what unexplored spaces lie between them? The answers will not come from a single study, a single book, or even a single generation of performers. Instead, they will emerge from continued inquiry, fearless experimentation, and the willingness to step beyond what is known—into the vast, uncharted potential of the human imagination.

References

Assagioli, R. (1974). The act of will. Penguin Books.

Assagioli, R. (1975). Psychosynthesis: Height psychology—Discovering the self and the self (An interview conducted by B. Besmer). Psychosynthesis Research Foundation.

Assagioli, R. (1976). Jung and psychosynthesis. Journal of Humanistic Psychology, 14(1), 35–55. https://doi.org/10.1177/002216787401400104

Baer, R. A. (2003). Mindfulness training as a clinical intervention: A conceptual and empirical review. Clinical Psychology: Science and Practice, 10(2), 125–143. https://doi.org/10.1093/clipsy.bpg015

Barnhofer, T., Duggan, D., Crane, C., Hepburn, S., Fennell, M. J. V., & Williams, J. M. G. (2007). Effects of meditation on frontal alpha-asymmetry in previously suicidal individuals. NeuroReport, 18(7), 709–812.

Battista, J. R. (1996). Abraham Maslow and Roberto Assagioli: Pioneers of transpersonal psychology. Textbook of Transpersonal Psychiatry and Psychology, 10(2), 52–61.

Bishop, S. R., Lau, M., Shapiro, S., Carlson, L., Anderson, N. D., Carmody, J., et al. (2004). Mindfulness: A proposed operational definition. Clinical Psychology: Science and Practice, 11(3), 230–241. https://doi.org/10.1093/clipsy.bph077

Brown, M. Y. (1983). The unfolding self: Psychosynthesis and counseling. Psychosynthesis Press.

Cahn, B. R., & Polich, J. (2013). Meditation states and traits: EEG, ERP, and neuroimaging studies. Psychology of Consciousness: Theory, Research, and Practice, 1(S), 48–96. https://doi.org/10.1037/2326-5523.1.S.48

Chew, P. G. L. (1995). Aikido politics in interview interaction. Linguistics and Education, 7(3), 201–220. https://doi.org/10.1016/0898-5898(95)90023-3

Chiesa, A., Calati, R., & Serretti, A. (2011). Does mindfulness training improve cognitive abilities? A systematic review of neuropsychological findings. Clinical Psychology Review, 31(3), 449–464. https://doi.org/10.1016/j.cpr.2010.11.003

Claire, E. B. (2016). Effects of acute exercise, mindfulness meditation, and mindfulness meditation neurofeedback on Stroop performance [Doctoral dissertation, ProQuest LLC].

Cortright, B. (1997). Psychotherapy and spirit. SUNY Press.

Donald, T. S. (1986). Aikido, a systems model for maneuvering in mediation. Conflict Resolution Quarterly, 1984(14). https://doi.org/10.1002/crq.38919871410

Duke, B., Sperling, M., & Kapsali, M. (2016). Answer the question. What are your/the tools of training? Theater Dance and Performance Training, 7(1), 108–111. https://doi.org/10.1080/19443927.2016.1149365

Dykhuizen, C. J. (2000). Training in culture: The case of aikido education and meaning-making outcomes in Japan and the United States. International Journal of Intercultural Relations, 24(6), 741–761. https://doi.org/10.1016/S0147-1767(00)00029-8

Eddington, S. A. (1984). Quantum questions: Mystical writings of the world's great physicists. New Science Library.

Einstein, A. (1979). Albert Einstein: The human side. Princeton University Press.

Ernest, G. H. (1991). The spiritual discipline of aikido: Its religious aspects and psychodynamic value. Journal of Pastoral Care & Counseling, 45(2), 127–132. https://doi.org/10.1177/002234099104500204

Faggianelli, P. (2006). Aikido and psychotherapy: A study of psychotherapists who are aikido practitioners. Journal of Transpersonal Psychology, 38(2), 159–178.

Farb, N. A. S., Anderson, A. K., Mayberg, H., Bean, J., McKeon, D., & Segal, Z. V. (2010). Minding one's emotions: Mindfulness training alters the neural expression of sadness. Emotion, 10(1), 25–33.

Frankl, V. E. (1975). The unconscious God: Psychotherapy and theology. Simon & Schuster.

Frankl, V. E. (1978). The unheard cry for meaning: Psychotherapy and humanism. Simon & Schuster.

Frank, J. L., & Jeffrey, M. C. (2008). Work in the 21st century: An introduction to industrial and organizational psychology. Personnel Psychology, 61(2), 447–450. https://doi.org/10.1111/j.1744-6570.2008.00119_2.x

Fromm, E. (1961). Psychoanalysis and religion. Yale Press.

Goleman, D. J., & Davidson, R. J. (1977). The role of attention in meditation and hypnosis: A psychobiological perspective on transformations of consciousness. International Journal of Clinical and Experimental Hypnosis, 25(4), 291–308. https://doi.org/10.1080/00207147708415986

Grof, S. (1976). Realms of the human unconscious: Observations from LSD research. E. P. Dutton.

Harris, A. R., Jennings, P. A., Katz, D. A., Abenavoli, R. M., & Greenberg, M. T. (2016). Promoting stress management and wellbeing in educators: Feasibility and efficacy of a school-based yoga and mindfulness intervention. Mindfulness, 7(1), 143–154. https://doi.org/10.1007/s12671-015-0451-2

Kabat-Zinn, J. (1994). Wherever you go, there you are: Mindfulness meditation in everyday life. Hyperion Press.

Kabat-Zinn, J. (2003). Mindfulness-based interventions in context: Past, present, and future. Clinical Psychology: Science and Practice, 10(2), 144–156. https://doi.org/10.1093/clipsy.bpg016

Wilber, K. (2000). Integral psychology: Consciousness, spirit, psychology, therapy. Shambhala Publication Inc.

Wong, Y. S. (2015). A randomized, controlled clinical trial: The effects of mindfulness-based cognitive therapy on chronic insomnia among Chinese patients in the community. Integrative Medicine Research, 4(1), 34–45. https://doi.org/10.1016/j.imr.2015.04.366

Appendix A: Script of Scene 1 of Act III in Hamlet

Monologue of Hamlet

Original text:

> To be, or not to be: that is the question:
> Whether 'tis nobler in the mind to suffer
> The slings and arrows of outrageous fortune,
> Or to take arms against a sea of troubles,
> And by opposing end them? To die: to sleep;
> No more; and by a sleep to say we end
> The heart-ache and the thousand natural shocks
> That flesh is heir to, 'tis a consummation
> Devoutly to be wish'd. To die, to sleep;
> To sleep: perchance to dream: ay, there's the rub;
> For in that sleep of death what dreams may come
> When we have shuffled off this mortal coil,
> Must give us pause: there's the respect
> That makes calamity of so long life;
> For who would bear the whips and scorns of time,
> The oppressor's wrong, the proud man's contumely,
> The pangs of despised love, the law's delay,
> The insolence of office and the spurns
> That patient merit of the unworthy takes,
> When he himself might his quietus make
> With a bare bodkin? who would fardels bear,
> To grunt and sweat under a weary life,
> But that the dread of something after death,
> The undiscover'd country from whose bourn
> No traveller returns, puzzles the will
> And makes us rather bear those ills we have
> Than fly to others that we know not of?
> Thus conscience does make cowards of us all;
> And thus the native hue of resolution
> Is sicklied o'er with the pale cast of thought,
> And enterprises of great pith and moment
> With this regard their currents turn awry,
> And lose the name of action.—Soft you now!

The fair Ophelia! Nymph, in thy orisons
Be all my sins remember'd.

Modern text for reference:

The question is: is it better to be alive or dead? Is it nobler to put up with all the nasty things that luck throws your way, or to fight against all those troubles by simply putting an end to them once and for all? Dying, sleeping—that's all dying is—a sleep that ends all the heartache and shocks that life on earth gives us—that's an achievement to wish for. To die, to sleep—to sleep, maybe to dream. Ah, but there's the catch: in death's sleep who knows what kind of dreams might come, after we've put the noise and commotion of life behind us. That's certainly something to worry about. That's the consideration that makes us stretch out our sufferings so long. After all, who would put up with all life's humiliations—the abuse from superiors, the insults of arrogant men, the pangs of unrequited love, the inefficiency of the legal system, the rudeness of people in office, and the mistreatment good people have to take from bad—when you could simply take out your knife and call it quits? Who would choose to grunt and sweat through an exhausting life, unless they were afraid of something dreadful after death, the undiscovered country from which no visitor returns, which we wonder about without getting any answers from and which makes us stick to the evils we know rather than rush off to seek the ones we don't? Fear of death makes us all cowards, and our natural boldness becomes weak with too much thinking. Actions that should be carried out at once get misdirected, and stop being actions at all. But shh, here comes the beautiful Ophelia. Pretty lady, please remember me when you pray.

Appendix B: Script of Scene 2 Act III of Romeo and Juliet

Monologue of Juliet

Original text:

> *Gallop apace, you fiery-footed steeds,*
> *Toward Phoebus' lodging. Such a wagoner*
> *As Phaeton would whip you to the west*
> *And bring in cloudy night immediately.*
> *Spread thy close curtain, love-performing night,*
> *That runaways' eyes may wink, and Romeo*
> *Leap to these arms, untalked of and unseen.*
> *Lovers can see to do their amorous rites*
> *By their own beauties, or, if love be blind,*
> *It best agrees with night. Come, civil night,*
> *Thou sober-suited matron, all in black,*
> *And learn me how to lose a winning match*
> *Played for a pair of stainless maidenhoods.*
> *Hood my unmanned blood bating in my cheeks,*
> *With thy black mantle, till strange love, grow bold,*
> *Think true love acted simple modesty.*
> *Come, night. Come, Romeo. Come, thou day in night,*
> *For thou wilt lie upon the wings of night*
> *Whiter than new snow upon a raven's back.*
> *Come, gentle night, come, loving, black-browed night,*
> *Give me my Romeo. And when I shall die,*
> *Take him and cut him out in little stars,*
> *And he will make the face of heaven so fine*
> *That all the world will be in love with night*
> *And pay no worship to the garish sun.*
> *Oh, I have bought the mansion of a love,*
> *But not possessed it, and though I am sold,*
> *Not yet enjoyed. So tedious is this day*
> *As is the night before some festival*
> *To an impatient child that hath new robes*
> *And may not wear them.*

Modern text for reference...

(...Juliet enters alone)

I wish the sun would hurry up and set and night would come immediately. When the night comes and everyone goes to sleep, Romeo will leap into my arms, and no one will know. Beauty makes it possible for lovers to see how to make love in the dark. Or else love is blind, and its best time is the night. I wish night would come, like a widow dressed in black, so I can learn how to submit to my husband and lose my virginity. Let the blood rushing to my cheeks be calmed. In the darkness, let me, a shy virgin, learn the strange act of sex so that it seems innocent, modest, and true. Come, night. Come, Romeo. You're like a day that comes during the night. You're whiter than snow on the black wings of a raven. Come, gentle night. Come, loving, dark night. Give me my Romeo. And when I die, turn him into stars and form a constellation in his image. His face will make the heavens so beautiful that the world will fall in love with the night and forget about the garish sun. Oh, I have bought love's mansion, but I haven't moved in yet. I belong to Romeo now, but he hasn't taken possession of me yet. This day is so boring that I feel like a child on the night before a holiday, waiting to put on my fancy new clothes.

Appendix C: Results of Participants for Two Performances

Evaluation Scores of Participants

Participant No.	Group No.	First Performance	Second Performance	Result
01	1	2	5	+
02	1	3	6	+
03	1	5	7	+
04	1	7	9	+
05	1	5	7	+
06	1	3	2	-
07	1	5	4	-
08	1	4	6	+
09	1	3	7	+
10	1	5	9	+
11	2	3	5	+
12	2	5	7	+
13	2	4	7	+
14	2	5	9	+
15	2	6	9	+
16	2	2	5	+
17	2	3	7	+
18	2	7	6	-
19	2	5	3	-
20	2	6	7	+
21	3	4	6	+
22	3	6	9	+
23	3	4	9	+
24	3	5	6	+
25	3	8	9	+
26	3	5	5	/
27	3	3	8	+
28	3	4	3	-
29	3	5	4	-
30	3	6	9	+
31	4	3	5	+

32	4	4	6	+
33	4	6	8	+
34	4	4	8	+
35	4	7	5	-
36	4	4	3	-
37	4	5	8	+
38	4	7	6	-
39	4	5	7	+
40	4	8	5	-

Results of Evaluation Score in Groups

Group No.	Participants No.	Quantity of participants	Quantity of "+"	Results
1	1-5	5	5	100%
1	6-10	5	3	60%
2	11-15	5	5	80%
2	16-20	5	3	60%
3	21-25	5	5	100%
3	26-30	5	2	40%
4	31-35	5	4	80%
4	36-40	5	2	40%

Appendix D: Results of Participants for the Questionnaires

Results of Relative Confirmed Answers for the Questionnaires

Participant No.	Group No.	Quantity of 3,4 or 5	Results
01	1	8	+
02	1	7	+
03	1	9	+
04	1	7	+
05	1	9	+
06	1	6	+
07	1	5	/
08	1	6	+
09	1	6	+
10	1	7	+
11	2	8	+
12	2	8	+
13	2	7	+
14	2	6	+
15	2	6	+
16	2	2	/
17	2	8	+
18	2	2	/
19	2	5	/
20	2	6	+
21	3	4	/
22	3	8	+
23	3	9	+
24	3	9	+
25	3	9	+
26	3	5	/
27	3	8	+
28	3	4	/
29	3	5	/
30	3	6	+

31	4	9	+
32	4	8	+
33	4	6	+
34	4	9	+
35	4	7	+
36	4	4	/
37	4	5	/
38	4	7	+
39	4	6	+
40	4	8	+

Note: The "+" represented the proportion of the quantity of the choice "3,4 or 5" in all choices in the questionnaire was more than 50%; the "/" represented the proportion which was equal or below 50%

Results of Questionnaires in Groups

Group No.	Participants No.	Quantity of questions	Quantity of choice"3,4 or 5"	Result
1	1-5	50	40	80%
1	6-10	50	30	60%
2	11-15	50	35	70%
2	16-20	50	23	46%
3	21-25	50	39	78%
3	26-30	50	28	56%
4	31-35	50	39	78%
4	36-40	50	30	60%

Appendix E: Questionnaires for Participants

Participant No.

Please check the following 10 questions and give us your answers. Please note:

1- highly unconfirmed

2- not confirmed

3 - confirmed

4 - relatively confirmed

5 - highly confirmed

1. A kind of spiritual experience and power which could not be expressed by words during the performance.

1	2	3	4	5

2.Transcending spirit encourages me to think about the role-making while performing.

1	2	3	4	5

3. I'd like to play the role once again as now I realize how to play it better.

1	2	3	4	5

4. While performing, I was losing the feeling of space, time and the script, not sure where did the support strength come from.

1	2	3	4	5

5.I feel more acute about the role-making in the play, including the vision sense, auditory sense, tactile sense and so on.

1	2	3	4	5

6.A free feeling comes out while playing without affect of other things

1	2	3	4	5

7. My consciousness achieved a state which are much different from that in the normal state.

1	2	3	4	5

8.I could almost see myself from the second or third visual angle while performing, and I am seeing myself playing on the stage

1	2	3	4	5

9. It seemed that more feelings could help me how to show the role better to the audience

1	2	3	4	5

10. I have realized my fault and weakness in the performance at the one moment and tries to adjust it during the performance.

1	2	3	4	5

www.ingramcontent.com/pod-product-compliance
Lightning Source LLC
Chambersburg PA
CBHW022050020426
42335CB00012B/633